The Most Terrible Time in My Life

…Ends Thursday

Remedy Robinson

Dedicated to the poetry of Elvis Costello

Thank you for always filling

the darkest and lightest places

Prologue

Midnight: that inky, indeterminable time assigned

to the darkest and most quiet time of night. Earlier, when

the sky still clung to the dying August evening light, I'd

gone to bed confident, knowing that the next morning's

problems were all figured out. Before the Earth could right

its own ship and sail into daylight once again, however,

another problem arose. Without forethought or explanation,

I dreamt I was in a darkened hallway; I was feeling a bit ill

and making my way toward a nearby bathroom. The flip of

the switch that brought the harsh fluorescent light sizzling

to life turned my unfocused eyes to mere slits, suggesting

this might not be a dream after all. The indistinct figure that

came into sharper focus sent a jolt of terror ricocheting

around the walls of my heart as my knees buckled and I

crumpled to the floor.

There was a girl. A girl! Just standing there. Staring. I had no idea who she was or how she'd gotten in, or why she was even in the bathroom. A quaking heap, I was certain she was there to do me harm. I could neither move nor cry out for help; I could only make myself as small and as invisible as possible. How much time would pass there on the floor? I had no idea. Cowering and sick, straining to hear even the faintest sound that might indicate her departure, it felt as if I could remain there for an eternity.

Courage, like clarity, however, comes in spurts, and is fleeting at best. Each time I felt a surge of bravery, I'd peek my head around the counter to see if she'd gone. Each time, I'll be damned if she wasn't still there. Her eyes were dark and fixed right on me, unwavering. The terror returned. Over the course of what could have been an hour, or maybe just a few minutes, every time I looked, there she was, staring. She didn't speak, but did mouth each of my words in a time-delayed, out of sync mocking sort of way, as I managed in a quiet voice to ask if she would please leave. I knew it wouldn't have seemed obvious to her that I'd grown weary of this sort of strange incomprehensible torment, but I was still naïve enough to try. I was a twelve-year girl who was no longer a child, but a girl who'd never really been a person at all.

It's difficult to say, but perhaps the morning sun had begun trickling in. Maybe it was light that helped me to see that, all along, my captor was not really a captor at all. If only she'd been a figment of my problem-solving imagination, I might have understood this better, but no. She wasn't a figment; she wasn't a ghost; she wasn't even a real person. All this time, I'd been held hostage by what I finally realized was my own reflection gaping back at me from the bathroom mirror. I'd never seen this version of myself; so wild-eyed and confused. No wonder I didn't recognize myself. Understanding that it was my own reflection in no way made it easier to look at. I'd always

been told how ugly I was, but never knew I was *this* ugly.
So, I dropped my eyes, and, on hands and knees, crawled to
the toilet, where I sat, safe from that alien girl. Shaken,
drenched with adrenaline and smothered in self-animus, I
sat leaning forward with my elbows on knees and my
throbbing head cradled in two trembling hands.

     Barely perceptible at first, like a hearing test, there
began a low murmuring sound that gained in volume until
it nearly turned deafening. It was as if an airliner were
barreling down a runway and picking up speed in order to
leave this Earth. I looked up to see mom, fully clothed,
standing in the bathtub next to where I sat recovering. Had
she been there this entire time? Why hadn't she helped me?
Before I could fully form this thought, however, to my
eternal embarrassment, a man materialized next to her, a
man I'd never seen before. I couldn't hear what they were
saying over the din, but could plainly see they were
engaged in some sort of conversation, gesturing toward me

as they did so. The mortification flushed my cheeks and slammed my eyes shut as I reflexively propelled my arms down to pull my pajama bottoms up. In opening one eye enough to see that I'd failed to pull them down in the first place, I noticed as well that my unwelcomed visitors were now gone, the roar fading along with them, leaving me in stupefied silence.

I suppose I went back to bed after that. It was midnight once again as far as I could tell. I've no recollection of anything else out of the ordinary happening that night. Even after being held prisoner by my own distorted reflection, I still had little inkling of how harrowing the next few days were going to be. Unwittingly, I'd managed to solve the next morning's problem, just not in the way I had intended.

It was morning now. The Caseworker arrived as planned. I'd been assigned to her after my criminal dealings from the year before. Her role was to see to it that I re-

integrated into mainstream society after those terrible

things I'd done. Usually, the Caseworker would pop her

head in the front door, ask if I was behaving, then be off to

her next case in a flash. Today, however, she was all the

way inside the house, having come to escort me to my first

day of seventh grade. She and mom stood there, their

features darkened by the high desert late summer sun of

Salt Lake City that shone brightly, spilling in through every

crevice, creating halo shapes around the furniture and the

figures standing before me. It was as if the shadowy events

of the night before never happened.

But, my shirt *was* on right, I kept saying. I could

plainly see it was. Why were they saying it was inside out

and backwards? Why were they asking if I was on drugs?

Ever since I stood in front of that judge the year before,

when he looked down from his perch and asked if I were

promiscuous, I'd been subjected to many imponderable

questions that seemed to come straight out of nowhere. I didn't know what *promiscuous* meant, but had the good sense to suspect it was something I was right to deny, which I did quite firmly, just as I was doing now with these crazy drug allegations. Annoyed by this bewildering, endless line of questioning, I left mom and the caseworker standing with their featureless faces ballooning larger and wider in the living room, and stumbled my way into the kitchen.

Over the sound of my emphatic yelps of "get it off me, get it off," I thought I heard the Caseworker say something about not being able to "deal with her" as the front door opened and closed, presumably sending my court-appointed overseer off to meet with the next juvenile delinquent on her list. I didn't mean to cause a scene or make her leave. Screaming seemed a perfectly reasonable reaction to having a skeletal chicken wing fly out of the garbage can and land on one's shoulder. Instead of brushing off the horrifying little demon, as I begged her to do, mom came in and merely laughed derisively. But she wasn't one to laugh at anything; nothing ever seemed amusing to her. But, no, for the last time, *no*, I didn't know what acid was, let alone take any. All I took before going to bed last night were my hay fever pills. That was all, I swear.

How many pills did I take? Well, when you put it that way, it becomes an entirely different story altogether.

Here I was, a tattooed "ex-con" with a funny accent and stories to tell that no middle school kid should ever hear, let alone have been witness to, facing the humiliation of having to start at yet another new school where I knew I didn't belong. Far too much had happened to ever go back to school again.

So, if a normal dose of hay fever medication made me sleepy, I reasoned, then downing the entire bottle would make it so no one would be able to wake me, thus excusing me from the first day of what was sure to be another unbearable exercise in ridicule and rejection. I'd then wake up whenever the pills wore off, probably around noon, and simply run away again. I'd run away before; it was something I was not very good at.

By mid-morning, not long after the Caseworker had left, as mom did her best to stifle her laughter, nothing had gotten back to normal. She probably shouldn't leave me alone like this, mom reasoned, but didn't think taking me to a hospital would teach me the right lesson, so instead she took me to the reception area outside of her office, where I was told to wait. A little black Cocker Spaniel dog with floppy ears ran under a desk. It bared its strange yellow teeth and snapped each time I reached down to pet it. It took a few attempts at making friends with the little dog before realizing it wasn't a dog at all; it was someone's purse.

It was now clear that I'd been reduced to a mere spectator, forced to watch my own punishment from far outside the realm of my own comprehension. What had started by not recognizing my own reflection had now left me cut off from knowing who I was at all. Running away would have to wait until I could separate the peculiarity of these hallucinations from the nightmare that had become my actual reality. It would be years before I would understand that Benadryl, the name for my hay fever medication, while rare, when taken in large doses as I had, had the ability to create these horrifying hallucinations. That, and I never had hay fever to start with.

Hours and myriad imaginary sights later, a woman came in and asked what sort of brat I thought I was for demanding she close the door quicker so the chicken wing skeleton wouldn't be able to fly back in and land on my shoulder again. With a grand sweep of her arm, mom greeted the woman, leveled an accusing finger my way, and in a breathless voice exclaimed that, yes, *this* is what she had had to put up with.

Chapter One

The flight from Tampa to Chicago arrived a little ahead of schedule. A member of the flight crew escorted me to the gate where the final leg of the trip would eventually spit me out in Salt Lake City. The hallucinogenic hell that would mercifully end three days after it had gripped me in that bright bathroom was still more than a year away from this lonesome two-hour wait that lie ahead. I sat watching two boys playing on the escalators.

My dad and his new wife, Mary, dropped me off at the airport in Tampa, Florida that morning. I'd gotten home from school the day before expecting to be at school again today, but found my bags packed instead. This was a strange turn of events given that I didn't even realize mom was even still alive, evidenced by how all of her angry long distance phone calls had stopped some months ago. But

Mary said I demanded to go live with mom, so off I went.

Dad draped his arm around Mary's shoulder as she dabbed

at the tears welling in her heavily made-up eyes. She'd

caught a laughing fit when I asked why saying goodbye

was the only time people ever hugged.

Hand in hand, dad and Mary left with nearly a full

hour before the plane was scheduled to take off, giving

them plenty of time to return, to take me home to Mary's

house where we all lived. The flight finally boarded, the

doors were closed in a safe and professional manner. If

they were to come back now, it would too late. My fate, to

coin a cliché, was sealed. I was ten years old at the time.

There was no way I could have guessed that within six

months, shortly after my eleventh birthday, I'd be arrested,

indelibly marked, and sentenced for the unthinkable crimes

I was about to commit.

I was used to moving, used to change. I'd attended no fewer than eight different schools before starting the fifth grade, the grade I was now leaving without saying goodbye. My father, mother, older sister Cathy, and I moved at least twice a year as far back as I could remember. Moving around Tampa was one thing, but now long-distance travel was involved. It started when a friend of mom's moved, started his own company, and then offered her a job in a place I'd never heard, a place called Utah. Third grade had just ended, I'd just turned nine, when mom put my eleven-year-old sister and me in our father's charge as she left to set up a "brand new life" for us all in Salt Lake City. She'd send for us when she was settled, she said, and that it was going to be the most amazing place we'd ever lived.

That summer without mom was filled with swimming in the apartment complex swimming pool, eating popcorn for dinner, staying up late, and a bit of seemingly harmless mischief making. It was the summer

the old bristly bearded janitor let us take turns sitting on his

lap. The acrid smell of alcohol was overpowering as he

tried to kiss us. It was the summer I found a dead cat

without a head lying in the gutter and made a fool of myself

when I couldn't control my crying when I told my dad

about it the next day. It was the summer that was capped

off by the heavy dresser toppling over and smashing my

foot as I tried to find something clean to wear. I hobbled

my way to and from school that day, then slept in dad's bed

that night, knowing he'd make this excruciating pain go

away. When he finally got home in the small hours,

however, he ushered me back to the room I shared with

Cathy, where I was forced to sleep on the floor, unable to

climb up to the top bunk of our stacked beds. He promised

to take care of it "tomorrow." He didn't. I thought I heard a

lady's voice as he left without saying goodbye a few hours

later, around dawn that next morning.

It went on like this well into autumn. Mom was still in Utah, still getting settled. Dad came home every once in a while, but was usually somewhere else. The physical pain, the near molestation, the unexplainable gruesome sights, and even the runny eggs Cathy cooked for us that I never could stomach, all seemed normal. It was the life we'd always known. We were well into our first month back to school, the fourth grade for me and the sixth for Cathy, when mom decided she'd settled in well enough, that it was now time for the rest of us to make the long road trip to our new lives she'd created for us in Salt Lake City. Another school year, interrupted. It was life as usual.

Chapter Two

My dad was a locksmith by trade, but had lost his business a few years earlier when the Tampa Downs dog track had been robbed late one night. As the one who'd installed the safe that the burglars were able to crack "far too easily," he became Suspect Number One. That was his term, "suspect number one." Before the sun had come up Cathy and I were plucked from our beds by dark figures early one morning when I was four years old. We were then corralled on the living room couch for the next few hours. Police officers, maybe seven or eight in total, had stormed our house. The sound of closet doors sliding open, of contents of drawers being dumped out onto the floor, rang throughout the house.

When the rummaging sounds stopped, we watched as the handcuffs tightened around dad's wrists that he'd obediently placed behind his back. He was no stranger to trouble, he told us after he was released the next day on bail, but swore, with a wink, that he had nothing to do with the events of that night at the dog track.

He'd go on to eventually be cleared of all the charges, but not before spending a day or two on the front page of the local newspaper. This enhanced his tough guy persona, sure, but damaged his good reputation as a respected locksmith, thus leaving him to find a new profession. A ninth-grade dropout, it seemed his options were few.

Taller than some men but not as tall as others, likewise with his weight, my dad had wavy black hair, deep set brown eyes, and a permanent scowl fixed on his olive complected face. He wasn't a particularly friendly or even-tempered man, quite the opposite, really. Charming when he wanted or needed to be, yet most of the time it was as if his pin had been pulled and Cathy and I were left waiting for the exploding shrapnel to strike us. He never laid a hand on us, mind you, he never needed to; the balled-up fist

gesture proved sufficient motivation to either stop or start

whatever command he spit at us through gritted teeth. To

hear him tell it, you'd think Cathy and I were little more

than wild banshees with no redeeming qualities other than

our ability to bring him his cigarettes, he was a four-pack-

a-day kind of guy, or to pour a tall glass of iced tea when

he bellowed for us to do so; half ice, a little sugar, no

lemon, but make damned sure the sugar is just right.

Not that there were many, of course, but no family

outing was ever complete without hearing something about

"turning this damn car around" at least twice. Now that the

car was packed and heading out of Tampa, out of Florida,

on our way to Salt Lake City, the standard threat had been

amended to the promise of leaving us by the side of the

road in Mississippi or Louisiana if we misbehaved.

Hunkered down as low as I could go on the back seat,

careful to not meet dad's disapproving gaze in the rearview mirror, or risk incurring his wrath in any respect as he drove fast, fast as if he had an angry purpose, I spent the next five car-sick days in frightened silence. I had no idea what Georgia, Texas, or even Arizona looked like. Autumn in Utah, however, looked, felt, and sounded nothing like Florida. People spoke funny. There were no palm trees. The air was dry and stung our cheeks. Mountains jutted up with what appeared to be snow on them. Or maybe those were simply clouds? As dad told me years later, he got there, took one look around that "awful Mormon infested place," knew it wasn't the place for him, and "got the hell out of there."

Less than a week after he'd driven us into town, we were back in the car, this time headed for the airport, dad still driving with that same angry purpose. It was "for work" and he'd only be gone "a little while," he explained just before he sprinted toward the gate where the flight to Tampa would take him away from Salt Lake City forever.

Forever, that is, save for one brief stint a little more than a

decade later, but I'm not sure if that really even counted.

Chapter Three

Those first days Cathy and I spent in Salt Lake City
with mom were days that only grew darker and colder. Our
first exposure to a winter with snow left our feet
permanently wet and our bodies chapped from the coldness
that broke through our laughable excuses for warm clothes.
Cathy and I started yet another school already in session. It
wasn't that making new friends was difficult; it was
impossible here in this strange land, so we didn't even
bother to try. The frequency with which we asked when
dad was coming back began to elongate. Mom often stayed
at her office late, so we typically had our afternoons and
early evenings to spend in relative peace. Cathy continued
to cook for us. I was learning to play the flute. I was getting
better. She was not. This brand-new life that mom spent
months engineering for us felt pretty much like the old one,

only now we were behind on the rent in a big house, instead of a small apartment.

A month or so passed like this, until one day, mom just didn't come home. We didn't bother to think much of it. Her disappearance had come on the heels of dad's long overdue phone call; the one where he dropped the bombshell that he wouldn't be coming back. Every night since had been spent crying loudly in the background as mom pleaded with him to return, just as she had coached us to do. For Cathy and me, having a night or two off from performing these pointless histrionics was quite welcomed, whatever the reason.

Soon, we'd come to find out that mom was in the hospital, "clinging to life." Cathy and I remained unalarmed by this news. Mom liked hospitals and would admit herself whenever possible. Upon arriving at her office earlier in the week, we were told, mom had apparently banged her head getting out of the car. This in itself was not news. She always did seem to be rather accident-prone. By early that afternoon, however, she'd been rushed from her office to the hospital by ambulance, paralyzed from the neck down, the cause of which remained a medical mystery.

As with the summer just a few months before, we were once again on our own. Cathy resumed the role of all around boss as we looked after ourselves. The flute had to be returned due to a few missed payments. I spotted another dead cat in a gutter, this time one with a head. I slept with the lights on, but made sure to not cry like a baby about it as I had with the last one. Mostly, Cathy and I spent our evenings as we always had, quietly watching television.

Chapter Four

It must have been sometime not long after Thanksgiving, sometime before Christmas anyway, when Cathy and I were taken to the hospital to say goodbye to mom. She looked so peaceful and content just lying there. In her paralyzed state, she wasn't able to hug us, so we didn't have to try to hug her back. I was nine and half at the time, too young to actively hate anyone, let alone my own mother. Cathy seemed to like her well enough, but there was no mistaking the distance we instinctively kept from her. Mom had had quite the life, or so they said. She'd lost not one, but two children before she met my father and Cathy and I came along; the details of their lives and deaths were shrouded in yet another mystery.

The first two years of Cathy's life, I heard whispered, had been spent living with dad's adopted parents in Florida while he and mom remained in

Washington, D.C., his hometown, where mom worked as a Registered Nurse at a psychiatric hospital for the criminally insane. I was born in Dunedin, Florida mere weeks after mom and dad were finally reunited with their toddler, Cathy. The reason for their relocation, or for why they'd spent all this time apart from her was never mentioned.

What I did know for certain was that Cathy and I, after more than a month on our own in Salt Lake City, had come to say goodbye to mom, whose condition showed no signs of improvement. We were going to go on our first plane trip later that day, and that before long Cathy and I would arrive back where we belonged, back in Tampa, Florida. We'd start a third and, hopefully, final school in less than a grade, and everything would be great again. It wouldn't matter if dad didn't come around a lot, or how bad his temper got when he did. We would once again be in the warm welcoming south, far away from the horrible cold of that oppressive valley.

I nearly burst with joy, but knew to contain my emotions, when I saw my dad standing at the gate waiting as we were ushered off the plane and back into the real world. The very next moment, though, as we first laid eyes on the lady standing there, a little too close to dad, Cathy and I both began to suspect our lives weren't going to be what we thought they were going to be.

Short and rotund, from behind Mary could have easily been mistaken for mom. Even from the front, these two equally squat, painfully average, heavy-set women shared similar protruding guts and comically large breasts. Instead of mom's plain red hair, specious green eyes, and pock marked cheeks, however, Mary sported fire engine red lipstick and sky-blue eye shadow under a heap of dyed jet-black hair that was teased, hair-sprayed, and piled strategically on her middle-aged head. The high arching penciled-in eyebrows and the shocking swath of rouge that rested on the thick pancake foundation gave Mary a theatrical look, not unlike that of a disgraced televangelist's wife. Without making introductions, dad gave us a quick pat on our shoulders as he took Mary's hand and gently guided her toward the exit, out to a car we'd never seen before, and into a small house where two children, a boy and girl, were sleeping. Their babysitter was paid and discharged for the evening. A little space off the laundry room had been converted into a bedroom with two single beds that Cathy and I would share for the next fifteen months. It would be the first time I ever lived so long in one place.

Chapter Five

My dad's name was Jack. We knew this because it was tattooed in faded blue cursive letters on his left forearm. It was the first word I ever learned to read. It was situated just below the equally faded skull and crossbones that he said he'd gotten just before he joined the Coast Guard as a very young man. Mary, whose name and association we were left to divine for ourselves, rather puzzlingly, kept calling him "John."

The sleeping girl's name, we were told later, was Prissy, and the boy was known as Blain. Not much younger than I was, yet there was something so much more childlike about them. Prissy was routinely dressed in frilly attire and was rarely without some sort of adorable ribbon in her hair. Blain preferred cowboy boots and would start crying if anyone dared to touch one of his many matching cowboy hats. Both seemed to be under the impression that they belonged there, that they weren't wild banshees. Their last name was different from mine, which was the same as my dad's. In fact, Blain was a "junior," which meant he must have been someone else's son. Dad and Mary weren't married yet, but when they were to eventually marry later that summer, surely Prissy and Blain would be dad's stepchildren, not his *actual* children, like Cathy and I were. So, why then, were they already calling him "daddy?" Cathy and I did not call Mary, "mom," nor would we ever. We called her by her first name, and she called us by our first names, at least at first.

While it was clear that dad had a certain "type" when it came to the ladies, the similarities ended at the mere physical between mom and Mary. Where mom spent more time and energy getting out of doing a job than the job itself required, Mary was a vain beautician who seemed to go to work every day without fail. She owned her own home, and never had a serious illness, phantom or otherwise. Her obsession with the pursuit of what she considered to be physical beauty was rivaled only by the adoration she had for her children, whom she doted on like no mother I'd ever seen before.

As we settled in to this new life, the one where dad came home every evening, it didn't take long before Cathy was dubbed "frog face," and I, "the mooch." Just as Cathy and I were unprepared for a life with Mary, it would seem Mary was as equally unprepared for our unplanned intrusion into the life she'd apparently been waiting years to finally live with a man we barely recognized, a loving father and husband whom she called "John."

As I would learn, or more precisely, piece together over many years while still not comprehending it all, dad must have known Mary for nearly as long as he'd been in Florida. Dad met Mary, he said, at a local coffee shop on one of those late nights after a routine locksmith call, a typical night when he didn't want to go home to mom.

Mary was married, unhappily so, or at least one might assume. Dad got her pregnant but didn't stick around, so she remained with her husband and had the child, whom she named after him. A year went by, and the same sequence of events unfolded yet again, this time reportedly producing Prissy. What happened to Mary in the intervening years between Prissy's arrival into the world and dad's return to Tampa from his brief stay in Salt Lake City, I couldn't say. I was having difficulty enough trying to wrap my head around dad's anger toward "that fat bitch" mom for demanding a divorce, when he was the one who'd left her, the one who'd left us.

Sharing the same last name with mom, who, as it turned out, dad was never married to, made as much sense as having to get a legal divorce from her, which was what he was forced to do now if he wanted to get married for real this time. I overheard words such as "common law," and how the State of Florida could not reverse my official birth status from "legitimate" to "illegitimate." So, after scores of angry long distance telephone exchanges, the paperwork was filed, the requisite waiting period was satisfied, and dad and Mary were finally able to get married, which they did without much fanfare. One day they came home, announced that they'd gone to city hall earlier in the day, and now they were husband and wife. That was the day dad got drunk and threw up in the bathtub. That was also the day I figured mom must have died, since her name was never mentioned again. Now we all had the same last name, the Giggle family, Jack Giggle, Mary Giggle, Cathy Giggle, and me, Georgia Gale Giggle; all six of us under that tiny roof of Mary's house. All of us, that is, except of course for Prissy and Blain. They still shared the last name of the man who assumed they were his children; the ex-husband who faithfully paid child support until the day each of them came of age, or so dad often bragged about. He always did love a good scam.

Chapter Six

Cathy wanted to go with dad and Mary, she said, when they dropped me off at the airport, but wasn't allowed to. Instead, she and I stayed up late that last night, chatting in the dark in our little space just off the laundry room. Mostly, Cathy kept asking why I'd ever want to go back to Salt Lake City, why I'd demanded to go live with mom. It seemed to not matter that I had demanded no such thing.

Sure, life as the proverbial ugly stepchild wasn't pleasant, and swapping an unpredictably absent father for one whose apathy was on permanent display seemed like a cruel trick to play on an unsuspecting child, but I loved fifth grade so much that it was simply unthinkable that I'd ever want to leave it. It was the middle of February; three more months and I would have the only uninterrupted grade I would have had the pleasure of attending. I adored our teacher, Mrs. Payne, and the knack she had for stirring

our imaginations as she read fanciful stories she'd written,

like the one about an adventurous little turtle named Liam.

I knew that one day I wanted to be a writer, that I wanted

people to hear my voice, just as we heard Mrs. Payne's. I

wanted people to see the worlds I could create, just as Mrs.

Payne had showed us hers.

I'd been placed in a "gifted" program at school that

dad grounded me for, thinking I'd been placed in some sort

of remedial class myself through sloth or some sort of

misbehavior. A blind boy named Dmitri, in the special

needs classroom I helped out in three times a week, printed

my name in Braille and placed them on all my books in

case I ever forget them in his classroom. That way, he said

proudly, he would know to keep them safe for me.

Occasionally, a girl named Alicia and I would walk

home together. It was as if I were starting to understand

how to make a friend. I was even working my way through

the beginning stages of my first crush on a boy named Todd Mulligan. He'd recently stabbed me in the wrist with a pencil when I kept reaching over to touch his elbow. The broken tip that embedded itself just below my skin was a thrilling little grey reminder of the attention I'd received from such a cute boy. I imagined the look of utter disappointment on Todd Mulligan's face when the news broke to a stunned Mrs. Payne's fifth grade class that their favorite student, and his future wife, was now sitting at an airport gate in Chicago, never to return.

Such gleeful thoughts, of course, were something I rarely dallied in. So, feeling stupid, for surely if my own father wasn't going to miss me, Todd Mulligan and Mrs. Payne weren't either. I turned my attention to some boys playing on the escalators as I sat waiting. At the very least, I hoped someone explained to Dmitri why I no longer came to his classroom. I would no longer be in his classroom, my classroom, my home, or even my state for, you see, I'd stolen from Mary, made fun of Mary, inconvenienced Mary. Cathy wasn't much better, but at least she showed an interest in hairstyles and makeup, at least she was old enough to babysit. All I was able to do was annoy Mary with what she considered to be my "weird brainy" ways. Yes, I was specifically told to not eat Mary's breakfast bars, the ones she said were for her diet, but I did anyway. Whenever I could pluck up the courage, I'd sneak into the kitchen while the rest of the house remained asleep, spirit a bar under my shirt, and eat it on the way to school. I knew it was wrong, I knew I was being a "mooch." Maybe it was that, or maybe it was when, just a few weeks earlier, Mary pulled my ponytail, called me a little bitch, and stormed off when I made fun of her middle name. But that's what we did; we made fun, or so I thought. Mary's middle name, *Lenore*, was equally as funny as me getting my first period, certainly. The ridicule I received from both Mary and Cathy was as merciless as it was difficult to understand.

These, and a million other thoughts of what else I could have done wrong and what I could have done better ran through my mind there in the Chicago airport. The flight to Salt Lake City was about to board.

Chapter Seven

After a marathon day of connecting flights, long
waits, and turbulent thoughts that refused to quiet, my
connecting flight from Chicago arrived in Salt Lake City. A
sea of people moved about, but mom wasn't among them.
An hour went by. No one came. I sat there picturing the
boys playing on the escalators in the Chicago airport and
how I envied the fun they were having running up the
down, and down the up. I wanted to try it myself, but was
terrified I'd get to the bottom of one escalator and not be
able to find my way back up somehow. I'd feel lost and
wouldn't know who to turn to, so I sat there quietly as I
was told to do. Now that I was back in Salt Lake City, a
place I didn't want to be, waiting hours for a mother I
didn't want to be with, I regretted not playing on those
escalators. If I were to have gotten lost there in the Chicago
airport, perhaps someone would have found me, taken me

to where I was supposed to be. Here in Salt Lake City, it'd only be a matter of time before I'd be lost forever, without anyone ever bothering to look for me.

Maybe if this were Mary's story, she'd sheepishly confess that she was a young mother and new wife at the time. Maybe she'd confess that she was overwhelmed by the installation of an instant family of four children, two of which weren't as angelic as her "real" children. Something had to give, and that *something* was a girl named Georgia Gale Giggle. Twenty years my father's junior, only thirteen years my senior, Mary was much younger than I could have ever guessed under all that gaudy makeup. Anyone, including myself, sitting there alone in the Salt Lake City airport, could have forgiven her had she just been honest. Her official story, unwavering and etched in stone, however, would of course be that it was my "bitchy demand" to go back to Salt Lake City, that she had no control over the decisions of a ten-year-old child.

Thankfully, mercifully, and, probably an even little vindictively, this is not Mary's story. She, her children, and even my own father, are bit players at best. This isn't my story either. Not quite, anyway. One day I hope to be important enough, to be loved enough, to just *be* enough to have a story worth telling. This story isn't about me. But like Mrs. Payne's story, it is by me. This is the story of how the most terrible time in my life… Ends Thursday.

Chapter Eight

Sixteen years old and doing my best to navigate the Chrysler Cordoba I'd stolen from mom through a snowstorm over a slippery mountain pass. This is exactly what was expected from a "bad kid" like me. Five years of detention, endless court appearances, foster homes, group homes, and various other forms of institutions and accusations nearly mandated that this was what was going to happen. No one would be surprised to hear what I'd done *this time*. Then again, nothing seemed to remotely startle any of us since having to identify Cathy's body. In the year since her death, when she was seventeen and I fifteen, life and loss, drama and chaos continued unflinchingly, as if actions had no consequences, as if there was still nothing to live for.

About a month after Cathy's closed casket funeral, the one where I'd reportedly made quite the spectacle of myself, mom opened a restaurant and threw herself headlong, tirelessly, into its day-to-day operations. Since moving to Utah, mom had started many businesses. And similar to all of her other endeavors that had gone under over the years, this one also found her surrounded by an adoring staff who were in awe of her courage and her resolute spirit. Naturally, the pity elicited from the unthinkable grief of losing a treasured child trumped the martyrdom of having an out-of-control *criminal* daughter to contend with, so I was pretty much left to my own directionless counsel during this time.

The head chef at mom's restaurant was a fun loving and wise man named Bob, whom she put all of her trust into. When the waves of sympathy began to crest for my now-beatified sister, mom turned to Bob, at her wits end, after reading in my diary that I'd been "making out" with a boy. Bob took me aside and, in due course, told me how much he loved me, then left to take a better job at a swanky ski-resort restaurant just over the hill east of Salt Lake City, one where the paychecks didn't bounce. Mom's restaurant would go on to close soon after that. Having a regular job was beneath mom, the boss and businesswoman, so it would only be a matter of time before she would find the next scheme to indulge her talents.

I tried reaching Bob at work, but a woman intercepted the call. He was "with her" now, she said, and no, there wasn't a message she would give him, especially one so "full of shit." What would a twenty-four-year-old man, divorced with two children of his own, want with a pimple like me? Her unsolicited advice was to stop playing games, run along to class little girl, and leave her alone to be with Bob.

But there was no game to stop playing. There certainly was no school to go back to. I'd not been in a proper classroom since the beginning of eighth grade, just before being sent away to a facility for out-of-control teens.

There was, well, there was nothing. I was officially a *nobody* in this world. If my novice driving skills were to somehow take me over this snowy mountain, if I were to somehow find Bob in the labyrinth of ski resort condos in which he was rumored to live, I didn't know what I was going to say, I didn't know what I was going to do. More than likely, I'd start with what I'd been conditioned to do: apologize. Ask for Bob's forgiveness. Not that my pleas for forgiveness had done me much good up till now, but ever since that day Mary put me on that plane to go back and live with mom in Utah, it was all I'd been doing.

Chapter Nine

The sun had long since set over the Great Salt Lake the day dad and Mary put me on that plane in Tampa. I'd sat there watching through the towering airport windows as the Utah sky turned from crisp blue to iridescent pink to slate grey, until finally, the moonless night turned the glass into an unforgiving mirror that left me with nothing to see beyond my own reflection.

Without any apologizes or excuses of her own, just a rebuke for not being where she thought I would be, mom finally found me waiting at the terminal gate, three hours after my plane had arrived on time from Chicago. With her usual halting gait that made others continually turn and wait for her, mom always seemed much older than her now forty years. As we stepped into the February air, once again I felt the unwelcoming sting of the Utah winter as it slapped my southern cheeks. Once again, I felt myself recoil from the touch of mom's pudgy hand as she pulled me close to welcome me "home."

The house where Cathy and I had looked after ourselves while mom lay paralyzed in the hospital wasn't the house where mom lived now. She'd since moved into a one-bedroom apartment in a sprawling complex on the upper east side of Salt Lake City known as "the bench." It was cramped and it was messy. Her work kept her far too busy, she said, but now that I was here, keeping the apartment clean would be my job. As far back as I could remember, it had always been Cathy's and my job to attend to mom's messes.

It didn't matter that the apartment wasn't in the same school district we'd been in when we were here before because mom had enrolled me in St. Ambrose, the private Catholic school that was a mere twenty-five-minute walk down the hill. Under the white blouse and pleated plaid skirt of my school uniform I wore an old one-piece bathing suit that was at least two sizes too small. As uncomfortable

as it was, it served the purpose of flattening my own

potentially comical breasts that had begun to burgeon much

earlier than it did for my fifth-grade counterparts. I looked

and felt stupid in this get-up that had me constantly pulling

the knee socks up over my chubby calves and worrying

about what would happen if I needed to use the restroom. It

would be the first time I actively dreaded going to school.

Uniform by definition I suppose, yet completely

different from the classmates I'd met that first morning, by

lunchtime, as I sat off to one side alone, I missed Mrs.

Payne and Todd Mulligan more than ever. Being neither

Mormon nor particularly Catholic, the exclusion from this

city I'd felt before was now squared. What started with an

occasional snowflake gliding harmlessly to the hard grey

asphalt as we crossed the courtyard from the chapel was

now beginning to transform into a swirling blizzard that, by the end of the day, turned my new world completely white and completely unrecognizable.

It was long past dark by the time I'd finally found my way up the hill to the apartment that was identical to endless rows of others, even when not blanketed by a foot of new snow. The flower pattern of my bathing suit now stood out clearly under my soaking wet uniform blouse. My fingers were too stiff and my socks were too wet to concern myself with their position. My hair, feet, and textbooks were all a soggy mess. Leaving school, I'd turned right when I should have turned left, only to realize after doubling back that I'd been going the right direction in the first place. It took more than a few attempts over what looked and felt like the surface of the moon to successfully orient myself.

Thankfully, it would be mom's Scottie dog, Mac, who heralded my close proximity by barking at the door that I soon realized I'd lost the key to somewhere along my pitiless trek. The sense of helplessness I might have felt waiting at the airport just a few days before was now a warm hug from a loving relation compared with the hours I stood at that door, angry and unprotected, frozen to the core. With each steamy exhale I could feel myself evaporating, my sense of individuality and purpose beginning to wither. The eternity spent standing there, knowing how much trouble I was going to be in, knowing I'd only have to do it all over again the next day, did little to endear me to this new situation.

Despite all the moving and family upheaval I'd accepted as "normal" in my scant ten or so years on this spinning orb, the sickening realization that things were only going to get worse pushed its way to the forefront of my addled mind. If not the prettiest girl, or the most popular, I'd at least always been the smartest girl, the "gifted" girl. Now, at St. Ambrose, it seemed I'd never be able to lay claim to that again. Mumbling my way through choral prayers in chapel was one thing, but the impenetrability of long division when even the simplest of multiplication problems confounded me, was a bad omen. You can't start at so many different schools without something like this liable to happen. Even if it were possible to catch up, it was obvious I was no longer smart. Bad things were going to happen.

Chapter Ten

A couple of months after that inauspicious first day,
mom and I moved into a little L-shaped basement
apartment on a street called Kensington Avenue in the
Sugar House area of Salt Lake City. Still just a twenty-five-
minute walk from St. Ambrose, only from the other
direction now, mom assured me that this particular move
had as much to do with us needing more room as it did my
"stupidity" of getting lost.

Our new landlady, an older lady named Bea, who
chain-smoked cigarettes and drank can after can of beer
daily, lived in the upstairs part of the house with her
granddaughter, Kristina. Kristina's parents had been killed
in a car crash. This, at once, explained why Kristina lived
there and excused both her "wild spirit" and Bea's nightly
slurred profanity-laced outbursts.

Having always shared a room with Cathy, and since I'd been back in Utah, having to share one with mom, I was thrilled to finally have a room all of my own. The only way to get there was through mom's room, but once inside I was able to close the door and spend time alone in the tiny corner bedroom that was all mine. There was a vague notion of safety, albeit a fleeting one. Being from Florida, where there was no such thing as a basement, the windows that were at eye level inside but level with the ground outside captured my imagination. Facing the corner of the room, to the left I could see the tires of the car parked in the driveway; to the right I could see the dirt that held the grass in the backyard. I got to know Kristina better when she showed me how to crawl out of these windows so as to avoid telling mom where we were going. We were only going to a nearby tangle of streams and caves that we called the "gully," but there was something adventurous about stealing away from our *captors*.

Blonde, with spindly bird legs and one front tooth that stuck out farther than the other, Kristina had an air of rebellion about her that seemed obvious yet somehow charming and forgivable at the same time. Small though she was, Kristina must have been around Cathy's age. She seemed to know a lot about everything. Not smart exactly, just overly worldly. Kristina was lucky; she didn't have to go to my school. She went to a school where she wasn't forced to wear stupid uniforms or do impossible math. Had we gone to the same school, we more than likely would never have been friends. But proximity gave her de-facto best friend status that I would quickly grow to regret.

Springtime, a season I'd yet to experience in this part of the world, had finally come to Salt Lake City. The walk to and from St. Ambrose wasn't as traumatizing as it had been in the beginning, which was a relief in the grand scheme of things, I suppose. But I'd given up. I didn't speak up in class, or have any friends, or even bother to complete my homework. I thought about my flute. It hardly seemed fair that I hadn't been able to keep it, but still had to go to a school I despised despite the delinquent payment notices that were piling up on the table just inside the front door of our little basement apartment, just down the steep steps on the side of Bea's house that mom had to take one at a time, both going up and coming back down.

The tattered bathing suit I relied on ripped when stuffing myself into it one time too many, leaving me braless, feeling fat and exposed. To make matters so much worse, my face had broken out with what had to be the most ghastly acne ever recorded, otherwise known as a few blemishes here and there. Flat chested and still pre-pubescent, Kristina took perverse pleasure in watching mom pin me down and pick at my face until it bled and I nearly cried. Kristina wasn't very much like Cathy. While I'd indulged in mischief with both Kristina and Cathy, it was Cathy who rarely told on me, and Kristina who always, happily did. For instance, Kristina and I had stolen a pack

of cigarettes out of Bea's cupboard and smoked them with

Kristina's friends over behind the Laundromat down the

street. When asked about it, Kristina said she didn't know

why I'd do such a thing, but promised she'd try to stop me

if I ever did it again. It should have come as no surprise,

really, that it was Kristina who led the search party,

consisting of herself and mom, to where I'd been hiding

that day I simply couldn't find the strength to drag my ugly,

stupid self back to that god-awful school. Kristina's

crooked and sneering grin beamed ugly and as hateful as

she meant it to when I finally emerged to face my

punishment.

Chapter Eleven

If I'd have been smart, I probably could have spent

the day behind the Laundromat, or down in the gully, but

this being the first time I'd ever cut school, I chose to stand

behind the water heater in the small utility room next to the

permanently cluttered and soured dishrag-smelling kitchen

instead. I'd discovered this magical space the time mom

stomped toward me with an old dirty pair of pliers that she

intended to pull out one of my loose baby teeth with. It was

a cramped, dark, and warm space with the added bonus of

being too narrow for mom to fit into.

As with every school morning, I tiptoed past my

sleeping mom in her room, brushed my teeth, dressed in my

uniform, and because she was never on a diet and therefore

never stocked up on any breakfast bars with which to steal,

I opened and closed the front door as usual to make my

departure; only this time I remained inside. I thought the

wild drumming of my heart would surely wake mom and give away my hiding place and ruin my plan, but she didn't stir. In fact, there wasn't a sound until nearly noon, when mom drowsily, and then more emphatically, cleared her throat so as not to sound as if the ringing phone was just now waking her.

Named after the darling curly-haired little dance- and songstress of her day, but with a different set of talents that she used to wow the world with, mom was a Registered Nurse and skilled saleswoman named Shirley. As dad so eloquently put it, Shirley could "sell shit to a sewer." Her own health issues seemed to greatly improve when she'd taken a job in Tampa enrolling future caregivers in medical assistance courses at a trade school. Mom was a natural fit and the first choice of Dave Hedderman, a man she'd worked with in that Tampa office. He'd gone on to start a similar school in Salt Lake City. Despite his best salesmanship efforts, however, the school was floundering, so smartly, he turned to mom for help. That was when she left Florida with the promise of a great new life for us all.

Across the street from where my parents had lived with my grandmother in Tampa, after leaving Washington, D.C. shortly before my birth, mom recalled the "lovely family" who lived there and who happened to be Mormon. Extrapolating that if one Mormon family was "this nice" to live around, then an entire city would certainly be a fantastic place to live. Without much deliberation past this one overarching assumption, mom, as we know, accepted Dave's invitation, and started two weeks later.

Dave was the one who was kind enough to drive Cathy and me to the airport after saying goodbye to mom at the hospital on our way back to Florida. He said he wouldn't have minded if we'd stayed with him and his family that month we were alone there in Salt Lake City, but there was the issue of Mac, mom's Scottie dog. Dave wasn't a "dog person," you see, so he hoped Cathy and I understood why we had to look after ourselves between mom's accident and our departure. Strangely, Mac stayed with Dave after we'd returned to live with our father.

Mom's initial diagnosis was eventually amended to "Acute Spontaneous Spinal" something or other when a large blood clot was discovered lodged in her spinal cord, blocking her ability to move or feel from the neck down. The daily blood thinners she now took and the eight-inch scar that ran from her hairline past the collar of her nurse's uniform down her spine, helped to corroborate her story that she wasn't faking it to force dad to return to Utah, as most everyone suspected she was. After the delicate surgery to remove the clot was successful, mom regained most of her mobility and won a small amount in damages from the doctor who had written "hysterical" on her chart when she was first admitted to the hospital after banging her head getting out of the car. This notion of free money would be a theme mom would return to many more times throughout her life.

Soon after the settlement, mom bought the business from Dave, and that's pretty much the last we ever heard from him. The rumor was he went into Real Estate and made a killing. From time to time, though, I wondered if Dave were to have known the unthinkable sequences of events his innocuous job offer ultimately set in motion, would he still have asked mom to leave Florida to come to Utah? If he knew, would Dave have felt bad that I was stiff and bored, trapped behind a dusty water heater for hours, now listening to one side of a phone conversation where mom was assuring whoever it was on the other end that she was going to kill me for cutting school as soon as she found me?

As mom, who wasn't at work, and Kristina, who wasn't at school either, stood there scolding me for skipping school, it was apparent that Kristina was not to be trusted and that the long hours mom spent at her office were but a mere fabrication from a fat lady who liked to sleep in. In the Principal's office at school the next day, it also became clear why my only punishment the day before had been to climb out the bedroom window and make sure the nearby gate was closed, regardless that I'd been told a hundred times before to *not* climb out the window. My mother could see, the scary-looking head nun told me, that I'd gotten my first period, but that it was no excuse to disobey the rules and not come to school.

Oh, my god, I thought. First, I was told it was I who demanded to go back to Utah. Now I was being told I'd cut class because of this. The rationales were beginning to stack up against my favor, leading me to wonder about my own motivations, my own sanity. Did mom really spend a half hour forcing me to climb out the window so she could pretend she'd seen bloodstains on my panties? Why couldn't she have just asked? Zooming right past bad grades, social exclusion, big boobs, and gross zits, mom chose to assume the *one* issue that wasn't an issue *was* the issue that prompted my decision to hide behind the water heater. What was this with my period, anyway? Mary and Cathy had taken such great pleasure in teasing me about it at the dinner table, with dad joining in on the laughter, that I assumed mom would do the same, so I never mentioned it to her. Now she was telling everyone I hadn't told her about it because she no longer had hers, a fact I was wholly unaware of. If a girl's period was so natural and not anything to be ashamed of, why then was it such a continual topic of ridicule and humiliation? Life was quickly becoming something other people lived and something I wanted nothing to do with.

A million miles away from where and how it had started in Mrs. Payne's class, with none of the real problems addressed, but the made up one reprimanded for, fifth grade eventually spluttered to its agonizing conclusion. And while unspeakable events were soon to

befall me, at least I never had to go back to damned St.

Ambrose again.

Chapter Twelve

My birthday is not the twenty-third of June, nor is it in July as dad asked if I was sure about when I'd corrected him once. My birthday is the twenty-fifth of June, much to mom's endless disappointment. Exactly six months from Christmas, I've no doubt that many others who share and celebrate this date find it charming in a rather silly childish sort of way. However, having been inconsiderate enough to arrive two days after mom's wonderful late father's birthday, by the time my actual birthday rolled around each year, there seemed to be less to celebrate and more to apologize for.

Despite the St. Ambrose debacle, I still wanted to write little stories, like Mrs. Payne, so I asked for a diary in the days leading up to mom's umpteenth retelling of how I couldn't have done this *one thing* for her, secondarily known as my eleventh birthday. Instead of a diary, I received a high-waisted pair of green shorts, mom's favorite color, and a gathering of Kristina and her three friends. They were the friends whom I'd gotten in trouble with for smoking behind the Laundromat with not long after moving into the basement apartment. There in the backyard they all sat, unfazed, mere feet from my bedroom window that the older boy, Chris Brown, had crawled into the week before while the other two boys watched as Chris held me down, pulled my pants off and, well, did something quite horrible. I didn't know boys were allowed to put their hands there. Please, let us leave it at that for now.

Kristina, that horrible little monster, had heard about what the boy did shortly afterward, when the laughing boys showed her where he'd vomited on the driveway after crawling back out of my window. She rushed in to find me hiding in my closet, and, with unmitigated giddiness, dragged me to the window where she pointed to the

physical evidence of how "gross" *everyone* thought I was.

I'd secretly called dad later that same day. It was the

first time we'd spoken in some time. No, I wasn't calling

collect, I assured him each time he asked. I just, well, I, um,

thought I could, you know, come back, and maybe, um,

live with him again. Could I, please? Unaware that any of

this had taken place, mom's repeated insistence that I try on

my present transformed into grating background noise as

dad's words continued to reverberate in my ear all these

days later. As dispassionately as if answering a passing

waiter who'd enquired whether he wanted more bread, in a

matter-of-fact tone, dad said no. No, I couldn't come back.

If "bad things" were happening, as I could only bring

myself to hint at, then it was my own "damned fault." What

I needed, he concluded before ushering me off the phone,

was to stop being such an ungrateful "brat."

More than likely, blatantly disobeying mom's direct order to model the ugliest pair of shorts I'd ever seen on my equally hideous body while this jeering pack of jackals looked on could be construed as me being an ungrateful brat. Dad must have been right; all these bad things happening *were* my fault. In what was probably a panic, feeling more overwhelmed than I ever thought possible, I eventually accepted the pair of shorts, but instead of going inside to change, I ran. I ran as fast as I could to the gully. There was a little cave there that I alone knew about, or so I thought. My plan was to hide there for a few days.

Chapter Thirteen

Attached quickly, handcuffs being clasped can sound like a wristwatch being wound, or a set of metal window blinds freefalling to their closed position. When one spikey tooth at a time is deliberately gripped around your 11-year-old wrists, as my first pair were, it can resemble the jangly anticipatory sound of an old rollercoaster chugging slowly up its first steep incline, just before the whooshing fall that is destined to follow.

Mom was there on the floor, a blubbering blob. The second officer was on one knee at her side, comforting her to no avail, her wails only increasing in vigor and in volume. With pleading eyes meant to convey a scream that this joke had gone too far, I willed her to make this horrifying police action stop. With one arm slung across her face, obscuring one eye, she glared back with the other, but didn't utter an intelligible word for want of what could be considered theatrical whimpering. I could feel the sense of anger expanding, filling the crevices where once only mere despair resided.

The peaceful days I'd envisioned spending in that little cave in the gully after I ran away on my birthday were abbreviated to roughly seven hours when the chilly night air and my fear of the dark proved too powerful to stave off any longer. Leaving those trouble-making shorts on the ground where I'd attempted to use them as warmth and cover, I made my way out of the gully's inky darkness and crept back into the little basement apartment to face the consequences of my actions. All the lights were out. The front door was locked. I felt a rush of butterflies pooling in the bottom of my stomach as I lowered myself through that damned bedroom window. Shivering despite being under the covers now, I didn't sleep at all that night.

In the seven days between my birthday and the cops now handcuffing and hauling me away, mom and I agreed: there *were* going to be "changes made around here." Whereas my unvoiced changes included less physical and emotional torment, mom's changes included more housework and less "backtalk." Being "willful," and having run away had put me on thin ice, mom warned ominously. She'd spoken with Bea, she said, and Bea was all too familiar with the signs of an "out-of-control" kid like me, so I'd better do as I was told if I didn't want to be in even more trouble.

In addition to sleeping in, as I learned that day behind the water heater, mom also liked to cook, eat, and begin projects. She was skilled in how to dirty every pan in the house, how to empty out a drawer, and even how to start a load of laundry. Cleaning up after herself and finishing these projects didn't seem to be high on her list, however, so she put those on my list of things to do. From a very early age, mom had taught both Cathy and me how to vacuum "her way," how to fold the clothes "her way," and famously, how to do the dishes "her way." Mom had an "I cook, you clean" mantra that didn't live on a two-way street.

In the days leading up to the big Independence Day celebration, mom had been more productive than usual, beginning meals in small pots that invariably had to be transferred to larger pots, baking bunt cakes that stuck to the pan, frying up Southern Fried Chicken as only she could, and then leaving everything in viscous, stagnant, and moldy smelling water "to soak."

The repeated threats to call the police if I didn't rewash the dishes to mom's satisfaction grew louder and more persistent by the minute, as if it were the only logical conclusion to this level of disobedience, until finally, we were toe to toe in the living room, grappling over the green receiver of the Bakelite desk model telephone. Everyone said she deserved better than a mouthy daughter like me. Bea told her she should've done this weeks ago. They all agreed, she said, she'd done her best, but that I was simply a bad kid who was going to get what I deserved.

In the half a minute it took to recognize the shear idiocy of this wrestling match, with an exaggerated gesture of "be my guest," I ceded the grip I had on one end of the phone's receiver, plopped down on the couch, and waited for the police to come and arrest mom for being too lazy to wipe her own smelly butt. The momentum had staggered her backwards; a shrill gasp escaped her mouth as she caught her balance and dialed the police. It began with labored breathing. By the time mom was able to spit out our address to the emergency dispatcher, she seemed to be hyperventilating and shaking uncontrollably. Near to hysterics though she was, she was able to announce, twice so as to be perfectly understood, that her unstable daughter had just assaulted her and was likely to beat her again.

Please hurry.

Chapter Fourteen

Please forgive me if this sounds indelicate, but my first bra was a size 32B. I know this because it was written in indelible black ink on the inside of the nearly threadbare dingy white bra that I struggled to clasp behind my back. The plain red t-shirt I pulled over the bra felt rough but comfortable. My shoe size was 5, likewise denoted by the same indelible ink on each white toe of the black Converse sneakers with frayed laces I'd been issued. They too were comfortable. And while I'd just pulled on my first pair of jeans as well, which also seemed pretty amazing, it was the bra I remained focused on. It was such a simple yet ingenious use of fabric, elastic, and hooks.

After the ride in the back of the police car, which seemed like forever but probably only took about twenty minutes, we arrived at our destination, the Juvenile Detention Center on the west side of town that mom said everyone called DT. There was no turning back now; I was actually being taken to jail, arrested for not doing the dishes. Is this what dad felt like when he'd been arrested for the dog track robbery? Would he be proud of me now if he knew?

A jarring buzzing sound indicated the heavy door that the two officers had led me to was now available to push open, placing liberty on the outside and me on the inside once it closed with a metallic scraping clank sound seconds after we passed through. Now safely "in custody," my handcuffs were removed with far less fanfare than when they were placed. I was led away to the girl's section.

It was a flat beige world of holding cells, uniformed officers, and what I imagined were scads of other criminals, just like me, although I was yet to see any. It was growing late in the evening of the beginning of what promised to be a very long and very spectacular holiday weekend. It wasn't just the Fourth of July holiday; it was the bicentennial anniversary of the day the United States gained its independence from the tyrannical British. The entire country would be celebrating two hundred years of freedom this weekend.

I was led into a small concrete room with a cubbyhole where my new clothes awaited me. I was patted down and told to *strip*. The impatient look that flashed across the female officer's face incapacitated my brain function. *You mean, take off my clothes?* Frozen, with my mouth wide open like a fool, I felt nearly as trapped as I did that day Chris Brown climbed through my bedroom window. The tight grip the officer formed around my arm with her hand and with a firm order to *do it now*, however, served its purpose, and snapped me into action.

Having successfully showered and shampooed with a special soap as directed, I was now dressed in my Detention-issued clothes and being led to what I guessed was my cell. The officer said nothing as I followed her through a series of corridors that were protected by more heavy doors, past a dayroom with couches and a television, and finally down another long hall that seemed to be a dead end. There were maybe twenty doors in total down this hall, ten on each side. My cell would be the third one on the left.

It wouldn't be like in the movies where the jailer opens the door, pushes the thug into the cell roughly, then slams the bars shut with a salty quip about cooling your heals or being sent up the river. No. There were no sliding bars, just another heavy door, this one with a small plastic window. The officer used one of the large skeleton-like keys on the ring that she kept grasped tightly in her hand. She used it to open the last heavy door I was to pass through that day. Wordlessly, she swung the door open far enough for me to step in, then simply closed and locked the door behind me, as if she'd done this a million times before.

The footsteps of the nameless, faceless guard echoed and receded down the hall as I drank in my new surroundings: an uncovered light bulb shone down brightly from the ten-foot-high ceiling onto a concrete floor and a concrete slab that was just wide enough to support its thin unmade single mattress. There was a tiny metal sink with a scratched metal mirror just above it, a three-foot concrete wall that separated the toilet from the rest of the room, and a tall, narrow window at the opposite side from the entrance of what I calculated to be maybe a ten-by-ten room. It was small, whatever the actual measurements were. Tripled-layered with bars, glass, and a heavy screen, the window looked out onto a large field of patchy grass that was hemmed in by a chain-link fence with coils of sharp looking wire at the top.

A twinkling darkness overtook the room as the bright overhead light died without warning, only to return as a dimmed red version of itself a few seconds later. I unfurled the folded sheet that sat at the end of the concrete

slab and set about preparing my bed for the night. I tucked

in each corner smoothly and evenly. The hard thin pillow

without a case remained unimpressed by the fluffing I'd

given it. Folded in half, it might make a good place to rest

my head. I placed my shoes neatly under the concrete slab,

but left the rest of my new clothes on, as much out of

comfort and convenience as modesty. If there were other

girls in nearby cells, I did not hear them. All was silent. I

laid on my back peering up at the red light as if it were a

distant star and I were in a clover-covered meadow on a

moonless night.

Towering fences, razor wire, locked and heavily

guarded doors, barred and sealed windows; it might have

looked as if I were the one who was locked in, but in

reality, it was the entire world that was now locked out.

Now there was little chance of hearing Kristina's insipid

cackle, Bea's nightly screaming, or mom's constant

badgering. There was no need to hide behind the water heater, or run away to the secret cave in the gully, or even fear my own bedroom. For the first time in the six months I'd been back in Utah, or perhaps for the first time in my life, I felt safe. If death were as relaxing and as inviting as the sleep I had that night, I would have happily invited it right then and there. Only, not even death could have found its way into that little fortified concrete castle.

Chapter Fifteen

Three long tables flanked the crowded and

windowless second floor room, forming a sharp version of

a U-shape. Evenly spaced chairs were dotted all the way

around them. A lecturer's podium was positioned near the

whiteboard at the front of the room, leaving what looked

like breathing space in the middle of the place that would

soon host the very first class of my very first semester of

college. With no need for a case worker or a court order

required this time, yet with that familiar and predictable

sense of impending doom, I entered the classroom feeling

as if I were about to be exposed for the fraud I most

certainly felt I was. A decade or so had passed since the

Independence Day weekend that ushered in what would go

on to be the first of my many incarcerations. A lot can

happen in ten years. And a lot did happen. The phrase

"nontraditional student," while accurate, as described by

Salt Lake City's Westminster College when they accepted

my application, nevertheless failed to adequately quantify

just how *non*-traditional the path was that I'd traveled to

this frightening yet ultimately joyous event. It was the same

unlikely path that brought me into a series of worlds I

barely knew existed, a path that would usher me into this

college classroom tonight, and a fateful path that led me to

a man named Tom.

Tom was my boyfriend. Oh, how that thrilled me to

say. This wonderful man was *my* boyfriend. He kissed me

at the door of the apartment we'd been sharing for almost a

year as I left for that first class. He squeezed me close and

wished me luck. His touch always made my heart babble

and my head fuzzy. We both knew I didn't deserve him,

which made his affection that much more exquisite in

nature. Such an intelligent, handsome, and well-raised man,

Tom was far above me in nearly every respect. Despite

being only a year older than I was, he was finishing his

second year of his graduate degree in an emerging field
called Computer Science at the University of Utah while all
I'd been able to accomplish up to that point was avoid
being killed, and registering for three classes, nine credit
hours in total, that would begin my own academic journey.
From this vantage point, I knew I simply couldn't compete
with, nor fully fathom, the sort of *real* life Tom had come
from. The love, the stability, the privilege and education
Tom had growing up in Philadelphia was akin to a glittery,
candy-flossed fairytale in my mind. His father had given
him a car while I struggled to make the payments on the
used car I paid for with a job I hated, a job that had nothing
to do with what I really wanted to do, which remained
writing stories, like Mrs. Payne.

    In direct opposition to Tom, who'd gone to a private
high school and lived in the dorm his first year away at
college in Delaware, I secretly took the high school
equivalency exam one day. I made sure to take it when

Tom was away, not wanting him to know that I'd lied about graduating high school, which he suspected, and rightfully so, that I had not, each time he asked, which was quite often. The question would come up whenever I knew something he didn't. He'd muse aloud how it was even possible, given our drastic educational inequities and all. My intrinsic knowledge, it seemed, should have been no match for his parentally funded pedantry. My only hope for a harmonious relationship with this soaring example of refinement and sophistication, I reasoned, was to rise to his level, to elevate my education to match the intelligence I suspected I had, an intelligence that had always been diminished or otherwise discounted. Was I a smart person? The consensus, having dogged me since St. Ambrose, seemed to be, no.

The classroom soon filled with similar looking people, in both age and apprehension, perhaps twelve of us in total. When it came my turn to introduce myself as we went around the room, leaving out the part about not

having been in a real classroom since the end of seventh

grade, I told my new classmates my name, that I worked in

a Soils lab, and that I lived pretty close; all of which was

true. Here in this English Composition class, there would

be no mention of detention centers, court appearances,

tattoos, running away, or even Bob for that matter. None of

that would be brought up. It was as if I had begun my

writing career right then by effectively revising a part of

my own story. A lie of omission is still a lie, however.

Our professor was a profoundly elegant and well-

spoken woman named Marianne. Standing tall behind the

podium, she had long blondish hair, flawless skin, and one

of those hyphenated last names that, coupled with her

impeccable dress sense, gave her an air of royalty. She had

advanced degrees in English, Shakespeare stuff mostly,

was married to a doctor, and even drove a darling little

Mercedes convertible. She taught us the value of trusting

our own words and how those words had the ability to be as serious or as playful as we commanded them to be. To hear this proper teacher describe in her highly polished speaking voice how some parents allow their children to *masticate* in public was like how I imagined a deaf person might feel upon hearing a bird sing for the first time. Bawdy but brilliant, Marianne helped confirm what I'd suspected all along; that words and phrases had the potential to someday, somehow be my savior. They were, after all, at times my only friends, the only things that couldn't be taken away from me. In this, my favorite class, I wrote essays about eating sushi for the first time, about a mal-functioned parachute I cut away from after jumping out of a plane once, and I even compiled a fairly comprehensive research paper on the pros and cons of testing level-four pathogens, the kind without known cures. Marianne marked up the comma splices and helped with paragraph structure, but mostly she made me feel as if my words mattered, as if someone were truly listening to what I had to say.

Toward the end of that first semester, with all three of my classes–the Composition class, the intro to Sociology class, and the computer competency class–coming to a close, and with the very real potential of receiving a perfect grade across the board looming on the ever-brightening horizon, I knew Tom couldn't help but be impressed. I wanted him to be as proud of me as I was of him. He'd successfully defended his thesis and would soon graduate with his Master's degree.

On the eve of our final Composition exam, Marianne invited the entire class, and our "significant others," to her house for a little celebration. Tom and I spent most of the evening sitting close together, holding hands, and listening attentively to Marianne and her husband as they read little stories about their adventures together. They were a beautiful couple who lived in a beautiful home. It was something I could easily imagine for the two of us.

I didn't typically wear my long brown hair down or bother to put on makeup, but did that night. Of course I wanted to look nice, but I also needed to conceal the bruise under my left eye that I'd gotten a few days before when I used the word *advocation*, when what I meant was *avocation*, as in I felt like writing could be my avocation. It was just another example of how smart I wasn't, and why Tom's punishment for thinking I could ever be smart was so easily given and accepted.

All my final exams that semester went on to end with a flourish. It should have been the boost in confidence I needed.

Chapter Sixteen

A week and two days after the party at Marianne's house, I struggled my way out of bed as usual, showered quickly, kissed Tom goodbye, and got to work at the dreary Soils lab. I wasn't particularly good at or overly enthusiastic about my job. It was a job that consisted of washing, drying, weighing, pounding, and even rolling clumps of dirt that the field technicians brought in for me to run tests on. In short, if you could do it to dirt, I did it to dirt.

In his contented slumber, Tom had muttered something about "at least" being able to do something that I didn't quite catch when my gentle kiss made him stir a bit, just before I left in a rush to get to work. A few minutes late nearly every day, it seemed I never could get to that job on time. Each day I made sure I had a novel excuse chambered, however, just in case anyone asked. No one ever did. I was mostly left to monitor and manage myself as I set about performing odd tests that I never bothered to fully understand the reason for, here in this large, drafty, and perpetually dusty industrial sized garage that I'd worked in for going on two years now.

Working on my own as I did, I had a constant stream of new wave music coming from the nearby radio to keep me company, and what happy company it was. I'd always been told what terrible taste I had and always felt stupid about it, or at the very least, self-conscious, so this unbridled indulgence, relatively free of judgment, was an unmitigated joy that some might call a *guilty pleasure*. Depeche Mode, Robin Hitchcock and the Egyptians, Suzanne Vega, and one of my particular favorites, Tears for Fears, "everybody wants to rule the world," sang out without threat of reproach, and helped me pass this monotonous time in welcomed solitude.

Mary, my stepmom, whom I'd not seen since the day she and dad put me on that plane ten years earlier, would often remark how terrible my style was when I still lived at her house. She'd even gone so far as to predicate, despite only being ten years old at the time, that I'd probably go on to marry an ugly man. And sure, some people might have made mention that Tom was a little funny looking, citing his gangly-large hands and feet, his patchy beard, his nerdy glasses that exaggerated his head but made his brown eyes seem dilated and slightly beady in nature, and especially his weird facial contortions that accompanied every slight exertion of effort, but I didn't see it. All I saw was the strength of a 20-mule team, a brain like Einstein's, and an exacting style I could only hope to emulate. I couldn't wait for the day he'd finally propose. It would be the day I'd send Mary his picture and show her how wrong she'd always been about me. I'd happily invite her to the wedding, of course. I liked to think of myself as someone who didn't hold grudges.

Tom had been acting a little strange, a little secretive lately, like a man planning to pop the question. I felt tingly with anticipation, overjoyed with wondering what romantic gesture he'd use when asking. After all, Tom was nothing if not romantic. I took a little break from washing a clay soil sample through a sieve to call Tom, as was our daily routine, to make sure he didn't oversleep now that he no longer lived the luxurious life of a graduate student and had to work for a living like the rest of us. I must have dialed wrong. We always paid the bills; there was no way our phone could have been turned off. Each time I redialed, however, the same outcome: *we're sorry, the number you have dialed has been disconnected or is no longer in service. Please check the number and dial again.* Shut up, you stupid lady. Don't tell me to check the number. Geez, even this robotic voice was accusing me of being stupid.

Leaving every soil sample in whatever state they'd progressed to before reaching that recording at least fifty times in the span of three, maybe four panic-stricken minutes, I raced home to find out what had happened in the scant three hours since I'd left. The couch was there. The little television was there. There was no sign of forced entry or fire damage. But everything else, I noticed as I burst through the door, Tom's desk, his books that there on the shelf, the kitchen table, and even the rickety old waterbed, were gone. Tom was gone.

Chapter Seventeen

One night, when I was seven, when we all still lived in Florida and dad still didn't come home much, mom ordered Cathy and me to our room, to go to sleep and not come out for any reason. We'd not done anything wrong past the usual transgressions, nor did we need to be up earlier than usual the next morning; it was just another daily ultimatum mom laid down that had begun sounding more like background noise than any sort of respected, or even reasonable, parenting parameter.

The admonition I received a few minutes later, the piercing *that's what you got for getting out of bed*, reached my ears as I stumbled down the hallway, moaning and crawling helplessly toward mom as she sat watching TV in the living room. The thought that she'd set a trap at our bedroom door in case either of us disobeyed this latest order, and how I'd been caught in that trap, weighed heavy on my mind as I sat there in the bright glare of the

emergency room waiting area later that night, my throbbing

foot soaking in a steel pan of warm water.

Immediately upon exiting our bedroom door,

defiantly, to ask mom a question, I felt the searing pain of

what turned out to be an unexplainable round and bloodless

puncture wound on the ball of my right foot. It would take

a few hours to get to the hospital, and a few more once we

were there, to determine that there was nothing the hospital

could do. I'd have to go home and wait until a doctor could

remove the foreign object that had penetrated my foot at an

angle and broken off deep in my flesh. The constant and

unrelenting pain from something I couldn't see lasted

through the weekend and well into the following week.

Masked but unmistakable, the glee I thought I heard

in mom's voice as she handed me off, trembling and

pleading, to a doctor who took me into a private room and

carved my foot open, was the same sickening glee I heard

in her voice now. As the full shock that Tom was gone was still sinking in, I'd stupidly called mom from a payphone to tell her what had happened. She was saying something about how I needed to be with her now, how I needed to "come home" for a few days. But all that came through the line was the dismissive refrain of how that'd teach me to not do as I was told when the doctor presented her with the jagged and bloody quarter-inch stump of a toothpick, a toothpick she had dropped and not bothered to bend to retrieve. That'd teach me to drag my feet, she remarked, when we finally found the other half of the toothpick tangled in the carpet, her smirk of amusement on full display. I'd since grown too old for her to call the cops and have me taken away, but clearly I'd never be too old for her to revel in my misfortune. My boyfriend had just dumped me in a fashion reminiscent of a death sentence carried out with a sharp, swift, and irrevocable Guillotine drop. To the outside world, right down to judges, caseworkers, friends, and even a few well-chosen psychologists, it would have sounded as if mom were merely comforting her distressed daughter, her angry, out-of-control daughter who'd once again gotten what she deserved.

Alone in what was once our apartment, left with only a towel to huddle under, for Tom had taken every sheet, blanket, and pillow, I curled up on the couch he didn't want, and turned on the TV that he'd also left behind. "Dog Day Afternoon" was on. It was a movie about a man so in love with a woman he robbed a bank in order to pay for her sex change operation. It was a movie I'd never seen before. 3 a.m. found me still willing myself to sleep. Much like Tom, it would be a sleep that refused to even speak to me, let alone soothe my reeling mind, or offer any sort of relief. There would never be any explanation. There would never be any apology. After all, it was obvious; Tom was just too good for me.

Chapter Eighteen

If your right palm itches, quick, spit on it, wish for

money, then rub it on wood to make it *good*, rub it on blue

to make it come *true*. Don't step over a person who is lying

on the floor. If you do, you must immediately re-cross

where you stepped in order to stymie the bad luck created

by crossing over them in the first place. Don't rock an

empty rocking chair, lest you open a portal for bad spirits to

descend upon your home. Just don't. Above all, don't use

angel as a term of endearment. God will punish you. That's

why mom's baby, David, her angel, died suddenly as he lay

in his crib sometime during the night long before I was

born. Anytime anyone uttered the word "angel," mom's

face puckered, her eyes narrowed, and her chin quaked as

she begged to never hear that term again.

A self-professed skilled Tarot card reader, junior

astrologer, and part time psychic, mom was a deeply

superstitious woman who was highly intuitive as well. An unavoidable product of the voodoo south she was raised in, perhaps. She said she could always tell what sinister motivation I had in mind, often bandying about the adage that "whistling girls and cackling hens always come to some bad end," typically replacing the word *whistling* for whatever egregious behavior I was exhibiting at the time: being willful, clever, rude, deceitful, or her favorite, ugly, "don't be ugly." When it was Cathy, and not I as everyone assumed it would be, who came to her bad end, I'd somehow taken on the role of mom's *rock*, or at least that's the word she used to describe me in the days following that late-night phone call, the kind that always seems to come in the middle of the night.

I was locked up somewhere when mom threw an ashtray at Cathy, told her she was no longer her daughter, and demanded she get out of her house and never come back. Cathy didn't argue. Cathy never argued. She did as she was told. No police needed to be called. She left and moved in with the family down the street, a family with a St. Barnard named Dandelion, and two small daughters who needed a babysitter. The only thing Cathy loved more than cooking was babysitting and big lovable dogs, so it was a natural fit. For five months she lived as a family member to Dandy, the two young girls, their mother, and the mother's boyfriend who was simply known as "Doc." Having served time himself, Doc earned his moniker through his discrete and skillful ability to patch up friends who'd been wounded in the commission of petty, and not so petty, crimes.

Cathy's last days on Earth coincided with my newfound freedom from yet another court-ordered juvenile center. She said she liked living down the street, but never said why mom disowned her, what made her return to Salt Lake City, or even why she'd done so in such a clandestine manner, stealing away early one morning without either

Mary or dad knowing. She'd remained in Tampa for a few years after I left, until she was around thirteen or fourteen, I think. Given how my life had been reduced to crossed-off calendar squares of days, weeks, or months to go before being released from some sort of incarceration, exact ages and dates had become difficult to pinpoint.

The years spent in what I imagined was her subservient role of Prissy and Blaine's handmaiden under Mary's passive aggressive Southern Bell regime changed Cathy, but not for the good, I thought. We were no longer allies. Raised in the same never-ending cyclone of chaos though we were, we had developed decidedly different coping methods and had personalities that were uniquely our own. Cathy still had our original southern accent that had long since been shamed out of me. She smoked Virginia Slim cigarettes like a cartoon aristocrat and refused to run away with me every time I asked her to. If I were the defiant, out of control, angry jailbird, then Cathy was the pitiful girl who never questioned why. Stubborn yet oddly non-confrontational, desperately shortsighted, and really quite clumsy, Cathy had grown into a rotund and reticent young woman whose lack of direction and education seemed to suit her well. Born on May Day, only seventeen years old, yet it was clear life had nothing left to offer her. She was laid to rest on a crisp and clear September day in 1980, in a grave with no headstone or marker, on a hill that would forever provide a stunning view of the entire Salt Lake City valley from the east.

Doc had only been in the store long enough to buy a pack of cigarettes and maybe some beer, he said, his voice strained, his words labored when he phoned with the news. But the blood, it was everywhere, emanating from somewhere on Cathy's head on her now limp body. He'd returned to the parking lot, to the car his friend was driving, an old prison friend who'd recently been paroled.

All he wanted was a kiss, *one kiss* the friend kept muttering as Doc urged him to drive faster in the direction of the nearest hospital. The force and velocity of the bottle he'd smashed into the side of Cathy's head, when she rejected his advances, rendered him dazed and her beyond mortal assistance. She was dead before the speeding car careened into a ditch, struck a tree head-on, and came to a mangled rest in an upside-down smoldering heap of tangled metal.

It is difficult to reconcile how, at that very violent and horrible moment, I'd been sitting at the kitchen table writing a story about a group of friends who made so much money shooting pool in their local pool hall that they decided to travel to different states to seek their fortune in even bigger pool halls. It was an adventure story about people who unwittingly rise above their stations and accidentally succeed when no one else thought they could. Writing this story made me feel happy; happy for the time in a very long time. But then the phone rang. I watched it begin as it usually did, with a heaving chest and sounds of hyperventilation as mom held the receiver in her now trembling hand.

Dad had an unlisted phone number, so the local police down in Tampa were dispatched to his house with the message that there was news he might want to know. Assuming it was just another one of mom's ploys, angry to have been bothered so early in the morning, dad's own words of *if something bad was happening then it must be your own fault* pulsed in my ears alongside his sobs that crackled over the line in a low murmur as I told him what had happened. It wasn't that I was holding it together so well for a fifteen-year-old girl in order to take on the role of *rock* for my grieving parents, far from it. On the contrary, I marveled at their obviously incongruous reactions. I wondered why mom wasn't happy to have gotten her wish of never speaking to Cathy again. I wondered if dad would have been this upset had it been me, given how easily he'd turned his back and walked away in the airport that day, how easily my own cries for help had gone unheard.

If anyone were to ask me how I felt at that moment, which no one did, I'd have said it was Cathy who was the lucky one.

Along with a heart-shaped piece of cardboard festooned with white and red carnations glued down to form a crude representation of a broken heart, Mary sent a note explaining why dad couldn't be in attendance at the funeral. She made no mention of Cathy, but did go on to explain how dad had recently undergone open-heart surgery after his massive heart attack earlier that summer. The distance, she concluded, was just too far for him to travel.

As two nearby men swooped to help mom back to her feet when she collapsed at the graveside, I followed her pointing finger down the hill to where the approaching figures of the limping Doc, his wife, and their children were drawing ever nearer. It wasn't *what* I said, but *how* I said it, mom contended, that made Doc recant the events of that awful night. It wasn't her command that Doc and his family be turned away from the funeral service in progress. No, it must have been my mouthiness when delivering mom's edict that angered Doc enough to let Cathy's killer go.

In the official and final report, there would be no mention of anything happening prior to a shadowy figure, perhaps a small dog or a cat, that had darted into the road, spooking Doc's friend, an admittedly rusty motor vehicle operator who'd been out of practice for the previous five years, causing him to swerve into the ditch and hit that tree. The estimated fifty miles over the speed limit warranted a citation, of course, but the driver went on to be released from all responsibility of Cathy's death long before his many broken bones mended. He was released from the hospital and back into the world without further punishment.

We moved soon after, not because we were five months behind on rent, but because mom couldn't bear living so close to people whom I'd allowed get away with killing her daughter. Mom retreated to her bedroom and didn't come out for weeks, not until it was time to announce she'd bought a restaurant. No longer the source of strength I'd been mere weeks before, I spent that time at a little desk in my room where I recommenced writing my story about the friends and their pool hall, a story that had somehow taken on a much more somber tone than it had begun with. God punishes those who believe they can be happy.

One month to the day after she passed, Cathy came to me in a horrifyingly vivid dream in the darkest part of the night. I saw her face as plainly as if she were actually standing by my bed. Even if I'd had my wits about me

enough to speak, she wasn't there long enough. She wasn't
there long enough for me to apologize for how I'd asked
Doc to leave her service and how sorry I was that no one
would be sent to prison for her senseless death. *Don't grow
up too fast* was all she said before disappearing as quickly
as she'd appeared. It was advice that seemed far too late to
heed, and a sentiment that was far too heated to share with
mom, for Cathy would never be able to grow up; a fact that
would cosmically evolve into being my fault. Like so many
other bad things in mom's life, it was my fault that Cathy
was no longer with us, my fault she was dead. After all, I'd
been the one who'd continually brought bad luck upon
mom.

Years later, when mom found out that I'd been
accepted as an English major at Westminster College, she
told me Cathy had come to her in a vision, revealing that
while I was the one "who might like to write," it would be

mom, and not me, who would go on to be famous for

writing.

Chapter Nineteen

There'd been no need for handcuffs this time, just an officer escort from my cell into the courtroom, since the juvenile detention center and its court were ostensibly in the same building. They were connected by a covered and secure concrete footpath that only took a moment or so to pass through. The other, more experienced girls I was housed with in A Block called it "Freedom Bridge" because it was the path that led to the people who decided if you got to go home or not.

I scrambled to find the nearest available seat when the judge ordered me to sit down and wait. His voice sounded loud and hollow, as if coming out of a loud speaker and not from his pursed mouth. He was a small-framed man with thinning grey hair and an oversized black robe who sat perched looking like some sort of medieval gargoyle. The hearing, he said, would begin as soon as mom arrived.

The long bicentennial holiday weekend I'd spent locked up hadn't been so bad. I'd slept well and I'd met girls who didn't seem like criminals. They were much like me, I thought, so it was possible I could have been wrong. While the rest of the country set off fireworks and waved American flags, I'd been given good clothes to wear, I'd been fed, and to my delight, I didn't have to do the dishes once I was finished. The other girls and I simply stacked our trays by the cafeteria door, then went back to the girl's section, "A block." It was there where we spent our time in the dayroom before returning to our individual cells later in the evening.

There was a row of shelves along one wall of the dayroom. It housed a good supply of books that we were allowed to choose a limit of three to take with us to our cell. There wasn't a limit, however, on how many scraps of paper we were allowed to scribble on. Once locked in, I'd pull the mattress onto the floor and use the concrete slab as a little desk. I'd then set about copying the words from a book in order to practice my grammar and my cursive writing. Even after the red night light came on, I'd continue writing little notes, addressed to God mostly, about how I enjoyed waving to the night officer who peered into each of our cells once every half hour, and how I understood why she never waved back. I also wrote how I understood that Detention was a place we weren't supposed to want to stay, but that it was okay if he wanted to keep me here a little longer.

The alternative, going back to live with mom in that horrible little basement apartment, soon became out of the question when a chorus of audible gasps rippled throughout the courtroom as the door opened and mom finally entered. I'd never had a prayer answered before; I didn't know all I had to do was write it down in order to make it come true.

Green, yellow, black, and seemingly every shade in between, the swollen bruise that dappled the entire left side of mom's face, from forehead to chin, convicted me right there on the spot. This was clear evidence of the vicious beating I'd exacted upon mom with the telephone receiver, and more than enough evidence for why I needed to stay locked up. She didn't want to mention it, but thought she should, mom added, that in addition to my disobedience and violent outburst, I'd also been caught smoking and seemed to act strange around the neighborhood boys.

Amid the many books there on the dayroom bookshelf, there was a dictionary that I could have used, but I didn't care to know the definition of *promiscuous*; I just knew it wasn't true. None of what mom had said was true. Well, except for the smoking part. Now I had two things in common with dad, a taste for tobacco and a criminal record. By the end of the forty-three days I'd go on to spend in DT that first time, we'd have a third thing in common as well, tattoos.

Two other girls had been kind enough to show me how to do it. We took the black tray from a watercolor kit, along with thread that we wrapped around the sharp end of a sewing needle, so we'd know just how deep to pierce our flesh as we created little designs. Since it was only watercolor and not actual ink, it would only be temporary, we reasoned. My left shoulder, forearm, and that webbing between my thumb and pointing finger; I tried to create a design in each of these places, but could only manage a few clusters of black dots in each location before the pain became too great and I abandoned the pursuit. Among the three of us, it was only Nadine Hooper who was badass enough to complete a design. I watched the seemingly impossible combination of joy and pain on her face as she created a large cross on her forearm.

Nadine was a tough girl who liked to play practical jokes. That's why she was here. An ice cream sundae dish had slipped out of her hand as she tried to throw ice cream on a girl for fun. Just like me, she'd injured another person and was now charged with assault; only for her it was twenty-four stiches on a girl's thigh, and not a bruise on a woman's face who was taking blood thinners, that did her in. Nadine eventually was sentenced to a group home around the time I was released from DT and sent to live with a foster family, a family who had been informed of my proclivity toward violence. There were hidden weapons in each room, the foster mother told me, weapons she could get to very easily if I so much as even thought about hurting anyone else.

In addition to the official list of offensives now on my permanent record, I had once again been a thief. I'd successfully walked out of DT wearing the bra they'd issued me. Maybe I wouldn't have been sent back to Utah had I not stolen Mary's breakfast bars. Maybe Chris Brown wouldn't have assaulted me had I not helped to steal Bea's cigarettes to smoke with him. Now that I'd stolen from the state, there was no telling what kind of trouble I'd be in.

My release from DT coincided roughly with the start of the new school year, sixth grade at a regular public school a few blocks from where the vigilant foster family also kept padlocks on most cabinets and doors throughout their house. There would be little chance of getting caught in another snowstorm or losing my way again from this distance. But there would be regular kids, there would be math, and there would be gym class at this school. The likelihood of seeing both the permanent black dots on my arm and the big letters written on my bra during the course of changing into or out of our gym clothes became a recurring and persistent image in my mind. The risk of being exposed as a thief, a mom beater, and a jailbird was too great.

On that hot late August morning, it was clear that I had no other choice. I left the foster home and walked toward the school on its opening day, then I walked right past the school, and then I just kept walking. And walking. There was no need to look back or reconsider my decision to simply leave. After all, I was a criminal. I knew very well that this was a criminal act I was committing.

My plan to go back into the gully and live in that little cave hit an unexpected snag when I realized there must be more than one convenience store like the one I'd always used as a landmark. To get to the gully, we'd always gone to the store with the sign, turned left, gone two more blocks, and the gully would be there straight ahead after you made a slight right. When following these familiar directions, yet on unfamiliar streets, led to places I'd never seen before, I just kept walking until I'd somehow found myself trundling along State Street. It was a long and wide boulevard that I seemed to recall being on before. My new plan was to follow this road until I found the convenience store I was familiar with, and then I'd once again be back on track. The thought of distancing myself from the constant scrutiny of those judgmental foster home strangers was exciting. The relief of not having to enter that new elementary school was liberating. Yet, the passing hours began to feel like days and the distance covered like mere blocks.

It must have been somewhere around the fourth or fifth hour into my fruitless quest to find the gully when, exhausted and frustrated, I took some of the coins I'd found on the ground along the way, plugged them into a payphone, and with tiny butterflies floating in my empty stomach, dialed the only phone number I knew, the number that would ring the green Bakelite desk model telephone I'd been accused of repeatedly beating mom with, the one that had hit her in the eye when I let go and she kept pulling. There was something oddly exhilarating, something pleasingly symmetrical about my words coming

through that very phone, asking in a dry and broken voice if

mom would please call the cops and have them take me

back to DT.

My punishment, however, would be much different

than I imagined it would be as I stood there at the

payphone, under a relentless sun, watching with nervous

anticipation for the approaching black and white police car

to arrive, anticipating the weight of handcuffs around my

wrists again, concocting excuses for why I'd stolen one of

their bras once I was returned to DT. It was a mistake, I'd

say. Someone told me I could have it, I'd say. I didn't

notice, I'd say. While all plausible lies, and despite being a

"bad kid," lying never came easily to me. I knew the right

thing to do was confess and face the consequences.

A few cabs mistaken for cop cars passed, but police

officers themselves never arrived. A car horn blew instead.

An arm jutted out of a driver's side window and waved me

over. It was mom, come to take me *home*. What I had done was wrong, but to end up exactly where I'd started, in that basement apartment, seemed like a tedious and needless turn of events. I'd run away from a court-ordered foster home, yet it would take another two days until I'd be back in detention; two miserable days filled with all that I'd since thought I'd be protected from. Two days when, what was billed as just another routine trip to the grocery store, turned into the pre-arranged hushed maneuver orchestrated by mom to bring me back behind DT's concrete walls, without, as she put it, *incident*.

This second stint in DT would be brief. It would be a mere whistle stop en route to my final destination, the psychiatric ward on the third floor of Primary Children's Hospital up on the hill on the east side of town. Her training as a clinical nurse helped her understand what was really going on, mom said, as if she herself were sitting behind that high judge's desk. To put it delicately, she said,

I was crazy and needed help. How else could you explain

an eleven-year-old girl who didn't like her own mother?

Chapter Twenty

Ninety days can go by exceedingly fast when you're having fun. Three months can go by fast when you're surrounded by pleasant people, doing new and exciting things; playing touch football out on the lawn, going to roller skating rinks, shopping for new clothes, or even visiting a movie theatre where g-rated films were shown. Still, what my time at Primary Children's Hospital couldn't do was pinpoint a cause for this aversion to mom, or find a cure for my insanity she insisted I was plagued with. I'd have happily stayed there on the "psych ward," living forever in this environment of hope and understanding, never once thinking of running away from this ironic bastion of sanity and calm. But sadly, no one was allowed to stay for more than three months. So, upon my release, I traded friendly nurses and trusted counselors for stoic nuns and stern "house matrons" at a boarding school just outside of Las Vegas, Nevada, called "The Home of the Good Shepherd." I'd opted to go there instead of returning to mom's custody. It was the right choice. It was the only rational choice. I'd be in the middle of the desert, behind tall fences, unable to run away. And sure, it was another private Catholic school, but at least I didn't have to wear a uniform at this one. Life at the Home of the Good Shepard was joyless and highly regimented. Even the classes, which I had high hopes of loving, were bland and uninformative, mere placeholders for the times in between church services and lectures on the evils of not living a clean and wholesome life.

Gone were the day trips and therapeutic activities. Gone were gentle voices and sounds of laughter. And even though it turned out to not be anything like I'd imagined it to be, I didn't regret my decision. I was away from both mom and Utah. The Home of the Good Shepard Boarding School for Girls was situated hundreds of miles away in the bare and sun-bleached desert on the outskirts of Las Vegas, the city mom called her most favorite place in the entire world. She must have told the story about how she and dad visited this magical city when she was pregnant with me at least three times on the drive down from Salt Lake City. A famous actor or singer, Robert somebody, had even rubbed a fifty-dollar chip on her belly for good luck as she stood at the Roulette Table. Or was it dice at a Craps table? With each re-telling, the details were always slightly different. I wondered how my parents could be in Las Vegas when Cathy was with our grandmother in Florida and they were said to be working in Washington, D.C. and unable to see her. There was something odd about so many of mom's stories. They just didn't add up.

Inside the living quarters at the boarding school, along a row of six-foot partitions that separated our little spaces, we each had a single bed and a chair that fit under the built-in desk next to the little built-in closet. Much like

DT, there were rooms on each side of a long and narrow hallway. Our doors, however, weren't locked. They weren't even doors, they were off-white stiff canvas curtains that hung from a rod that were to be pushed open at all times, except during our designated sleeping times. There was no talking allowed in the halls. No music other than what we were exposed to in the chapel was ever heard. There was a television in the common area, but it was strictly for special occasions only. In short, one melancholy day led to the next melancholy day.

About a month or so after I'd arrived, however, an unexpected wistful wave of nostalgia came over me as I set about doing my homework. I noticed the date I'd just written in the upper left-hand corner of my paper, *February Eighteenth*. I thought about Dmitri, the blind boy who was probably still keeping my books safe for me. I thought about Todd Mulligan. It was the one-year anniversary of when I'd travelled so unexpectedly to Utah, the day I sat waiting for mom in the airport for hours, two days before I'd nearly frozen to death trying to find my way home. 365 days away from Mrs. Payne's class, three million miles away from my sister and father. And now here I was, in Nevada, living on remote acreage where scorpions and field mice outnumbered people. I didn't like it there, but I didn't hate it here either. I feared it, as was the intention. It was going to give me the stability I'd never known. It was going to be the same school and the same living quarters for years to come. It was something I could rely on.

Chapter Twenty-One

Later that spring, mom drove down from Salt Lake City to visit. I wasn't allowed off the grounds, so after an hour or so of idle and forced chit chat, she left for the evening, promising to return the next day with watermelons and assorted other treats that I could share with some of my "friends," as if other remanded bad girls who just happened to live in the same hall could be considered, "friends." Kristina had taught me that the true meaning of a "friend" was someone you're never supposed to tell your secrets to.

More than an hour late, empty handed but with a bruise along the side of her right arm, mom arrived with the story of how she'd been mugged in her hotel's parking lot the night before. As the hotel security walked her to her room and brought her a soothing beverage, she said, that was when she had her epiphany.

It was difficult for her, she said, to be far away from me, so she knew it must be just as difficult for me to be so far away her. As a consequence, she decided that I needed to come home with her, to our new home that was no longer in a basement and no longer in the Sugarhouse section of town. It would be the house, a split-level duplex on a dead-end street, where, in four shorts months, I'd go on to be held captive by my own reflection and chased by that horrifying skeletal chicken wing during the days I'd be gripped by relentless hallucinations.

It wasn't until we were nearly halfway back to Salt Lake City, when mom mentioned that, of course, I'd need to be assigned to a caseworker and would have to begin seeing a therapist weekly. After all, there was still the matter of the assault, the question of my mental health, and how I never did finish doing my time in that foster home. This ludicrous cycle was going to continue like this for years. Nothing was going to save me from mom's whims.

I stared out the window in silence, watching the world go by, thinking about watermelon and how much I hated it. I'd hated it ever since mom forced Cathy and me to eat it in the bathtub when Cathy was five and I was three. I hated the sticky feeling, the unpredictable seeds that I'd accidently bite into, and worse, the smell of Zest soap and the scrummy ring it formed all the way around the tub in which we sat, scant inches from the toilet. The mere thought of watermelon was enough to turn my stomach and clench my teeth.

Three years later, less than five months after Cathy's death, when mom didn't show, and I was left waiting until long into the cold and dark of a January night at the alternative high school I'd enrolled myself in, I made my way three miles up the hill and over to our house, only to find mom sitting there, having forgotten all about coming to get me. Fed up with feeling as if she were trying to sabotage my life, but unable to say anything, for every time I expressed these thoughts to anyone, it was I who'd been sent for mental evaluations, locked away, or both, so I didn't say anything, I didn't retaliate. Instead, the next morning I took most of the money out of mom's purse and left. But instead of sleeping in parks as I'd done as a younger runaway, this time I was going to find a cheap motel room to call home for a few days.

More familiar with the city though I was since the day I left the foster home looking for the gully, I nevertheless wasn't quite sure where to find a motel. In just a few minutes, thankfully, it wouldn't matter. This plan would be scrapped without a second thought when I came upon a bus bench ad for a private driving school. For about the same money as I'd stolen out of mom's purse, they'd even pick me up. Repeating the seven digits as I dashed home until it sounded like a song, I was able to book a lesson and be outside waiting for my instructor before mom had even woken up. I was fifteen and a half; before long I'd graduate from *running* away to *driving* away. This was exactly the type of freedom I'd been looking for. It didn't take long to get my learner's permit. I was a natural. Driving was the single most exciting feeling I could ever have imagined.

And while mom let me use the car to go to the store or to run errands for her, she never did let me use the car to go back to that alternative high school, not even to retrieve the big bundle of notebooks containing the finished handwritten story of "The Pool Hall Friends," the story I'd finally finished and had asked one of my teachers to read for me. After all it had been though, the story probably wasn't very good anyway.

Chapter Twenty-Two

The skyline that rose up steadily before me, imposing though it was, wasn't quite as electric or as twinkly as I thought it be. Perhaps the five days of driving had somehow dulled my senses. Perhaps it was a little too real to actually find myself creeping along the George Washington Bridge, crossing into New York City, a place I'd always dreamt of going but never thought possible. That dream would soon be a reality as I rolled up to the toll plaza that was ablaze with artificial light in the cool but sticky early June night. After paying the three-dollar toll, my eyes readjusted to soak in the reality that would go on to last about an hour, or however long it took to find my way back out of the city and into New Jersey through the tunnel downtown. I just wanted to be able to say I'd been there, that I'd driven on New York City streets, taking in all its filth and loveliness, finally coming close to feeling like a member of the human race. If all went well, I'd be in Vermont tomorrow afternoon, a full day ahead of schedule. My new job would last until the first day of autumn and I was eager to get to it.

Having soldiered on with my classes at Westminster College after Tom left gave me the structure I needed, yet remained little consolation as I set about life as his cast-off ex-girlfriend, discarded like a doll with ratty clothes and chopped off hair. What Tom had done in the year following his hasty departure, what I allowed to continue to happen that year, was arguably worse than the initial desertion itself. Never minding whatever progress into adulthood I'd made, it was time for me to leave these circumstances and to run away again. Only this time, it needed to be as far as I could possibly go.

There were many types of far-flung summer jobs I'd considered. Cruise ship crewmember and Disneyland character were the obvious and traditional suggestions from classmates pondering their own summer adventures. But I didn't want obvious. I couldn't fathom traditional. I had a reliable car, a sizable tax return, and a summer break from college to go anywhere I wanted. I could have even retraced the road that dad, Cathy, and I had originally taken from Tampa to Salt Lake City, but the thought never even crossed my mind. The South, and Florida in particular, was out of the question. I simply wasn't welcomed there. I'd erased most traces of my innate Southern accent, not from assimilation but through necessity. Much like my ridiculously spotty and incomplete tattoos, my accent served as an indicator that I was different and therefore somehow defective; so long sleeves and a forced nondescript flat accent helped to circumvent scornful preconceptions as I evolved from that criminal kid into that heartbroken college student. Gone were my y'alls, soft vowel sounds, and the notion of any summer job that might reunite me with my white trash Southern roots.

Dad had an hourly mantra of, *what's wrong with you?* when he'd made his brief return to Salt Lake City, not long after I'd turned eighteen and was now considered an adult. Unable to yell and huff like he used to, dad was reduced to continual verbal jabs through gritted teeth to satisfy his need for anger. Everything I did, everything I said annoyed him. He noted with surprise how that "hillbilly-looking gap" between my two front baby teeth had thankfully closed now that my permanent teeth had come in. And while he didn't care for the scar it left, he said, he was glad to see I'd had that big dark mole on the bridge of my nose had been removed. It was a large and unsightly mole that started as a scratch from a cat we once had when I was in the second grade. After repeatedly picking at the scab the scratch had left, it turned into the permanent source of prominent disfigurement that not even Mary's greasy makeup could have covered. I tried to tell dad how the mole was so persistent that it grew back twice before the third painful removal from a sharp scalpel's blade ultimately left this preferable scar in its place, how I'd gotten it removed in successive, unexpectedly fortuitous, stints in DT from the ages of 12 to 15. "It made you look like a witch," he interrupted. With a cackle laugh like mine and that big wart-looking mole on my face, all I needed was a cauldron, he said, to become the fourth Gorgon sister.

My hair that dad had always insisted I keep short was now defiantly long, and he did not approve. It was messy looking and ugly. He said it was long because Cathy and I always wanted to look like the girls we saw on the reruns of "The Brady Bunch," when in reality it was because, well, I liked my hair long. He'd always had a way of making me feel stupid for liking what I liked, of making me feel inferior and a little crazy for loving what I loved.

It had been more than eight eventful and confusing years since dad and I had last seen each other; eight long years since he and Mary left me at the gate in Tampa. It was an event that I still viewed as my death sentence and was still quietly angry about, no matter how many times a parade of psychologists told me it was my fault and how I needed to accept it if I wanted to, as they said, *get better*.

Older of course, but not as old as I thought he'd look, dad now wore glasses and seemed less tall than he used to. His wavy hair was still thick, only less black and much more silver. A long pink scar that ran the length of his breastbone, the remnant of invasive lifesaving surgery, terminated just above his distended belly that was out or proportion with the rest of sturdy and lean frame. The scar served as corroborating evidence that he really wasn't lying about why he couldn't make it to Cathy's funeral, as I'd always assumed he was.

The three years since his heart attack had been difficult years, he said. We never spoke of Cathy, her death, or my enduring culpability, but Blaine had been arrested for stealing a little girl's horse and selling it to a glue factory. Prissy, who'd become a born-again Christian, was now a young married insufferable control freak who pressured him daily to accept Jesus, or else. And, added to the heart attack and resulting opened-heart surgery, Diabetes and Liver disease beset dad all at once, forcing him to go on disability. He was in constant pain and feeling like less of a man now that he was almost entirely dependent on Mary, whom he described as that *fat bitch* who begged him to stay as he packed his car to leave her and to once again drive to Salt Lake City.

The money mom had just come into, the luxurious house she was in the process of buying, and her exciting new business venture proved to be too strong of a siren song for dad to resist. He should have known it was all a lie. He knew she was a con artist *extraordinaire*. After all,

from what my grandmother had recently told me, that's

how they'd met in the first place. The sprawling house that

mom had described in detail to dad was still "in escrow"

and "not quite ready" when he arrived, so they had to stay

with me in the two-bedroom apartment I'd recently rented

using money I'd squirrelled away selling pot with an

absolute creep of a person, a violent man with a long

criminal record whose name I can no longer even bring

myself to utter. When you are young and directionless,

these are the kind of people who find you and tell you how

far beneath them you are. My first failed attempt to escape

his murderous clutches came in the form of a one-week

visit I made to my grandmother's apartment in her

retirement community, when I was 17 years old. It was

rumored that dad and Mary lived not too far away. I'd

flown down to Florida with the hope that I could finally

apologize to Mary for all that I'd done wrong and maybe

once again live with them. An immediate and wordless sound of the telephone line going dead was dad's response when grandma phoned to tell him I was in Florida and hoping to see him. The next long days were spent sitting by the phone, hopeful my dad would call, but the phone never rang there in my grandmother's little studio apartment. I took a taxi to the airport and once again steeled myself for the violence and debasement that had become synonymous with Salt Lake City.

Almost a year later, when the police surrounded the creep's house and he was arrested and taken away, my heart pounded with sheer joy. I knew this could be my only chance to finally get away from him. Thankfully, I was right. He went back to prison and was never again able to belittle me or chase me around with a loaded gun, shooting in my direction and threatening to kill me, mocking me for trembling and crying. This was the life I was told I deserved, but this was a ridiculous and hateful life that I didn't want to live in a second longer. I was free. From

him.

      The first thing dad said to me when he pulled up to

my apartment after his long drive was to make myself

useful and bring in his bags. There'd be no hello, and

there'd be no goodbye. Dad left my apartment and went

back to Florida as quickly as he could, presumably staying

as long as it took to realize mom had duped him again and

for Mary to wire enough gas money for him to make it back

home. He didn't have many years left after that, but the

years he had he spent with Mary. He and I had a long talk

once, not long before his end. He told me that Mary was the

only person he ever really loved. Knowing this meant that I

was among the millions excluded from his devotion;

understanding this meant there'd always be a hollow spot

where a father's love should have resided, that it was my

responsibility to fill it as I saw fit. He'd saved himself by sending me to Salt Lake City, and then saved himself yet again by returning to Florida, to Mary. They said his funeral was beautiful and that his grave was adored with a headstone with the song lyric, "always on my mind," chiseled in perfect script just above his death date.

Dad carried his own bags to the car as he left my apartment that night. I had little patience left for his rancorous disposition and was relieved to see him go. He probably wasn't even outside the city limits before mom spit on me, pulled my hair, and shouted how this was all my fault, that I had run dad off *again*. I spat back, shoved her to the floor, and may have even stepped on her a time or two as I made my way to the bathroom to clean up.

Leaving her in whatever heap she'd ended up in, I drove to the nearest convenience store and bought a newspaper in order to look for a job, a real job. I needed something. I didn't know what that something was, but knew that if my life were to continue, it was not going to

continue like this.

Chapter Twenty-Three

The graveyard shift, sitting at a bank of computers with a headset on, taking phone calls from insomniacs watching late-night television, fulfilling their orders for miracle blenders, magazine subscriptions, and the occasional charitable donation, that's where my new resolve had taken me. I didn't know how to type, but having the foresight to bring my own pen as I filled out the application landed me an immediate interview. I was hired on the spot. Training was from eight p.m. to midnight for a week, and then I'd move to my permanent shift of midnight to eight a.m. I couldn't throw mom out, she had nowhere else to go, but I could avoid her by sleeping all day and working all night.

The ten-year-old Pontiac Firebird that I'd recently been fortunate enough to buy was in decent enough condition, but was far too silly looking to command a steeper price, given how the seller had put bright orange doors on the otherwise dull brown car, so I got it on the cheap. I spent as much time just sitting in that kooky looking car and singing along with the radio as I did driving it. Bronski Beat's "Tell Me Why," INXS's "I send a Message," and Duran Duran's "Wild Boys," were among my current favorites. I liked my new job and I liked my new car. Not that these two items alone instantly made up for a lifetime of, well, whatever this life had been bereft of, but they were beginning to resemble some sort of a cosmic version of my very own personal elocution lessons.

And then, there he was, my new reason to continue. He was tall, slender, and sporting a set of vibrant blue eyes that complemented his boyish grin well. He approached with all the understated gunslinger swagger of Clint Eastwood, tapped on the passenger side window as I sat idling in a convenience store's parking lot, and invited himself to sit with me on a cold late December night. His name was Robert, he said. He too worked a late shift and was now headed home. His calm voice and pleasant demeanor caused two hours to evaporate as if they were made of mere minutes. We'd go on to have our first date a few days later; it would be my first real first date ever, a date filled with kindness and ease, not vitriol or hate. Robert came from a good family, the kind of family where the black sheep moniker was bestowed upon a mechanical genius who was nevertheless the only one of his four siblings to not go on to graduate from college.

They were the simple yet profound lessons that Robert taught me that meant the most. Fixing the bathroom door that wouldn't close all the way, as he did with ease and precision, without demand for payment or praise, showed me that kindness did abound, that there were solutions, and that we were able to mend the broken elements in our lives and not simply tolerate them as mere destiny. Encouraging me to fill my car's gas tank all the way, instead of limping by a few dollars at a time, helped me to see that I didn't have to live as if I were perpetually perched at the rim of a bottom pit, always bracing for the worst.

Robert's older brother was a geologist who worked in a lab that ran tests on rock core samples. The data generated from these tests were complex, but the procedures themselves were rudimentary. Objectively beneath the talents of the newly minted experts who'd taken the job in order to break into their chosen field with their shiny new bachelor degrees in hand. As a favor to Robert, who knew I could do better than a late-night order taker job, his brother arranged an interview for me. I was shown around the lab, taught the difference between sandstone and shale, and was introduced to a few hip and smart people who would soon become my new colleagues. Questioning their own career trajectory perhaps, though never outwardly begrudging my lack of experience, each of them were kind enough to walk me through each step of rock testing. I caught on fast, re-adjusted to a daytime schedule, and began to enjoy the spoils of personal growth wrought from the splendor of never-before-felt stability. Mom became increasingly unhappy with my new show-off attitude, audibly shocked that I was able to even keep a job. Her new business partner, she said, could also see how poorly I treated her, so they made arrangements to move mom into her own apartment, away from my abuse. The amount of people made from sheer trash who'd plagued my life was beginning to dwindle to a fairly manageable number. And although this would not be our final tousle by any means, I was still so very glad to see mom go.

As a material manifestation of the faith and confidence I'd earned, Robert cosigned a loan for a used but newer, pleasingly monochromic blue Toyota five speed. Even when the entire lab staff was laid off and I went a month before landing the soils lab job, I never missed a payment. The loan was paid off a year after

Robert and I broke up, marking what felt like the first time

I'd ever been able to keep a promise. I went on to buy an

even newer yet used Toyota five speed, a red one this time,

that I alone was entirely responsible for the repayment of.

Mentor and hero though he was, Robert and I, as the old

cliché goes, just weren't meant for each other. On the

dubious and unspoken anniversary of that first Fourth of

July visit to DT, for my criminal history was just that,

history and not spoken of, nine days after I'd turned twenty,

Robert and I went backpacking through the spectacular

Uinta Mountains. The three days spent far away from

modern conveniences such as a soft bed or a warm shower,

the two nights isolated from the rest of the bustling world

elated Robert as much as it depressed me. I'd long since

grown out of thinking that living in a gully would be fun. It

was obvious we both had much more living we wanted to

do, but had distinctively different views on what that life

should consist of.

Chapter Twenty-Four

Toward the sputtering end of my relationship with Robert, one day I just needed to get away. After putting in a full day at the soils lab, instead of driving home to shower and to call Robert, as was our routine, I just kept driving. Once a runaway, always a runaway. I drove until I found myself over the mountain and on the road heading into Park City. My driving skills and self-respect, I noticed, had come a long way since the last time I'd driven this route five years earlier, when I went looking for Bob.

A long line of cars slowed my momentum and piqued my interest. The singer Joe Jackson, the guy in the next car yelled over when I asked, was preforming an outdoor concert just up the road. The line, *don't you feel like trying something new* played in head as I pulled in with the rest of the concertgoers, bought a ticket, and quickly lost myself amongst the swelling crowd as the sun set and

the music began.

All that I'd gained, all the success I was feeling, had

been sparked by that chance encounter on a December

night when I didn't want to go home. It was the night I just

happened to meet Robert. For that, I'd forever be grateful.

Through the years, we'd go on to drift in and out of each

other's lives with all the ease, acceptance, and familiarity

of the sound of our own voices.

I'd go on to be a little less than eternally grateful,

but couldn't have guessed that at the time, when I spotted

Dennis, an old coworker from the rock lab, standing off to

one side of the crowd of dancing Joe Jackson fans. We

hugged excitedly, exchanged phone numbers, and spent

time together over the course of the next few months, until

he left to go to graduate school in Northern Utah. Much

like Robert, Dennis was also tall, blond, and from a good

family. Unlike Robert, however, Dennis lacked any

detectible charisma. Highly intelligent, adventurous, but just a little too weird, Dennis remained a *good enough* friend who always seemed to find a way to irritate me as I worked through my first adult breakup with Robert. Dennis favored terrible puns and the overuse of words like *hoser* and *geezer*; he breathed too loud through this nose, and worse, kept telling me who I was. Despite not knowing myself, I nevertheless took offense whenever he postulated that I probably enjoyed being chocked, or that I probably enjoyed pain, or that I probably was a screamer. All these *probablies* were most definitely off putting.

Dennis drove an unreliable old Volkswagen Beetle with a bright red lobster painted on the roof and two fish painted so the headlights were their mouths. It was broken down one Saturday when he wanted to go up to the drop zone, to a small mountain town where he and his friends gathered to go skydiving. Dennis was a friend who needed me, so of course I drove him up when he asked. Declining the offer to fly up in the Cessna to witness him jump out, however, as I was terrified of heights, I remained on the ground and watched with keen interest the process of parachute packing, parachute checking, and a succession of successful deployments and landings throughout the day.

Around dusk that evening, after all the jumps had been safely completed, we piled into a large booth with his friends at a local restaurant before heading back down the mountain. Dennis nestled in snug to my right, causing me to lean sharply to my left, bringing me shoulder-to-shoulder with a quiet bearded man. "I'm Tom," he said. It was no coincidence that I suddenly had an overwhelming desire to conquer my fear of falling.

Dennis went on to propose to a fellow grad student he'd recently begun dating, a diminutive Midwestern feminist firecracker, named Marybeth. Tom and I had begun living together in that small little apartment by this time, so Dennis stopped by to introduce his new girlfriend and to say goodbye as they passed through town, on their way to Illinois, where Marybeth owned a house just outside Chicago. She was already a successful computer scientist with designs on recreating Dennis in her image. She didn't like the way Tom, Dennis, and I seemed so familiar with each other, and the way, as she put it, I needed to be the center of attention, so Marybeth forbad Dennis to speak to me, regardless that it would only be possible through a long-distance telephone line from a half a country away.

Dennis and I called each other often after Tom's vanishing act. I couldn't tell if the glee detected in Dennis's voice originated from the thrill he got from disobeying the taskmaster Marybeth, or from the pleasure he took in me being dumped by the person I chose to date instead of him. The safe bet was two-to-one on either. He'd been cheating on Marybeth, he confided, with a woman who liked to be led around on all fours by a leash that she begged Dennis to attach to the tight-fitting collar around her neck.

Happier for myself to not have dated him than sad for the wife he was betraying, I concealed my disgust and tamped down any judgment, reminding myself that Dennis was a friend who just needed an understanding voice to confess to. The same consideration would not have been extended from Dennis to me, I was certain, if he had known that Tom and I had started seeing each other again, not in a dating sense, but in a pathetic *once-every-two-weeks-late-at-night-when-no-one-was-looking* sense. If only we could get back together long enough for me to dump him, I reasoned when these late-night trysts began, then this gaping wound would instantly mend and I could truly, as they say, "move on."

Toward the end of an entire year like this, however, my continued heartache paled in comparison to the cancerous self-hate I'd allowed to fester deep inside my worthless being. Tossing an idle and meaningless *I love you* my way as he left that last time was one of the cruelest things anyone had ever said to me. I drove out of town two weeks later, heading for the east coast, without saying goodbye to him.

Chapter Twenty-Five

I'd been reading Kerouac and Kundera in equal measures, convinced life really *was* elsewhere, dreaming of the Utopian existence out on the road where material possessions amassed were far less cherished than life lessons that left emotional and physical scars that were then worn proudly and without fear of reprisal. I chose the bucolic and remote recesses of New England to run to that summer. I'd found a job working as an assistant Innkeeper at the Silver Chalise Bed and Breakfast in a small town, somewhere in the middle of Vermont. What better place to live the reclusive life of a writer than in a small attic room three thousand miles away from anything familiar, anything hurtful? No experience was required, the owners assured me through our letters and phone calls that led to their job offer, just a good head on my shoulders and a desire to get my hands dirty was all I needed for this room and board off-peak season position. Dirt. If only they knew how sick of dirt I was.

Marcel, the male Innkeeper, was a Swiss-German Sorbonne-trained former flavor chemist who'd previously worked in New York City. He walked me through my first task, making toasted almond granola from scratch. Not bad but I could do better, he proclaimed. I scooped a handful into a plastic bag, sealed it up tight, and mailed it to Tom with a note that broke the news that I was gone. He wrote back to congratulate me; not for my successful escape, or for having bested him at his own deceitful game, not even for how delicious the granola was. As he sat eating, he wrote, he realized I'd found the perfect ruse in which to poison him with if I'd have wanted to. *But if looks could kill, there's a man there who's marked down as dead*, so sang Joe Jackson, and I was getting the feeling he must have meant Tom. Did it really take all these traumatic events, all this over-the-top heartache, and thousands of miles' distance to finally see that, all along, Tom might not have been the great man I thought he was, that I might have left behind far more than I'd been able to pack into one small car just to have one short summer away from his ghost?

In the time since I'd opened that apartment door to find Tom gone, it felt as if life had stood still, when in reality it had somehow kept going. I'd finally been laid off from the soils lab job that I hated. In the depths of my sadness, I was nevertheless savvy enough to collect unemployment and Pell grants as I lived the life of a real college student, binge drinking and trying to find a new group of friends of my own, accruing another year of college credits and maintaining a high GPA in the process.

The ensuing events of that summer would go on to ruin my life, or make my life complete, or a little bit of both, I don't know. I was 23, going on 24, and ready to start making mistakes based solely on my own poor choices and not merely the selfish whims of others. It was the summer of 1989 and what a summer it was. It'd be another two years before I made it back to Salt Lake City, another two years before I saw mom again. It would be another two decades before I finally earned my Bachelor's degree. It would also be another two years until I saw George Giggle, my son, again.

Born in 1982, just a few weeks after my seventeenth birthday, Georgie Dale Giggle was the message I'd tried to leave with Bob's new girlfriend when he worked at the ski resort restaurant. Bob never did return my call. Instead, I was at mom's mercy more than ever. Convinced that Georgie was, at once, the reincarnation of David and the way I could make up for what happen to Cathy, mom was the one who named him, the one who told me I had no "maternal instinct," and the one who set about proving that I was not only a terrible daughter, but now a terrible mother as well.

Thankfully, though, this wasn't mom's story. This hasn't been my story either. Not quite, anyway. One day I hope to be important enough, to be loved enough, to just *be* enough to have a story worth telling. This story isn't about me. This is the hopeful story of how the most terrible time in my life… Ends Thursday.

Chapter Twenty-Six

Bonus Material

"Loving Mother of Five"

A Short Story Concocted by Remedy Robinson

"It was so unfair," Mrs. Carlson said, pausing long enough to drag on her cigarette, long enough to exhale the spent grey cloud toward the heavens, and then draw in another clear, extended breath, deep enough to propel the words she'd been meaning to say in a manner befitting her eloquence. There had been a considerable silence before this utterance, of course. Some might call her style a flair for the dramatic, others melodrama, others still, the sorrowful lament of a wise owl, heartbroken and persevering. Some, like her assembled audience, had long since given up trying to describe what happened when Mrs. Carlson took the stage. "So unfair," she said again. It came out in a haughty stage whisper.

Gathered together in Mrs. Carlson's confined living room, her audience leaned forward, edging closer in anticipation as she repeated the refrain before continuing.

"It was so unfair that David's funeral had to be held on Sharon's second birthday," she said.

This was how the details of Mrs. Carlson's past, the details of her many children, mystery children most of them, were revealed: one small nugget of information doled out, one stuttered proclamation at a time, oftentimes contradicting what had already been revealed or whispered about before. This was 1992 in a town called Salt Lake City. Seattle's Space Needle was less than 1,000 miles away, and had been erected some thirty years before, just in time for the World's fair, just one yar after the one that had been held in Italy. Mrs. Carlson was a woman much older than her sixty-some years. It wasn't just her pockmarked face, or her saggy posture, or her dulled green eyes. She always did want to see the world, and it showed.

The audience, well sure, they'd known about David, or had at least heard about him. David was Ms. Carlson's third child by her first husband, a long-forgotten man named Doug. Not even pictures of him remained. David was her "angel" who'd died as an infant. SIDs, she'd say, never expounding upon what the initials stood for. A girl named Sharon, however, this was new information. It helped to shade in more detail, yet it remained a light pencil drawing at best. There was still the issue of the oldest child, rumored to be a boy, Michael, as well as a younger girl named Carrie. She'd been born after David, but when and to whom was as opaque as the details surrounding her death, for she had reportedly died as a child as well.

Four children: two dead (David and Carrie) and two lost somewhere in the world (Sharon and Michael). This number would rise to three dead and two lost, when Cathy, Mrs. Carlson's fifth child with her fourth husband, John, was beaten to death, murdered by an overzealous love interest. Cathy was laid to rest on a crisp autumn day in 1980. She was only 17. Grief. Loss. Tragedy. Strength. It seemed Mrs. Carlson's life had been filled with unspeakable events that should never befall a mother once, let only this many times. And the two missing children, Michael and Sharon, it should be stated, were snatched from her loving arms so heartlessly. What resilience. What grace.

What a load of crap.

Mary Virginia, Mrs. Carlson's younger sister, had flown in for Cathy's funeral. The family resemblance was nearly as strong as the tension that crackled between these sisters who hadn't seen each other since before Cathy was born. Both were short, squat Italian women with the same double chin and sloping shoulders. Only, Mary Virginia bore the correct pigment and eye color of her heritage, whereas Mrs. Carlson had red hair and those pale green eyes that kept losing pigment and depth. Those eyes would go on to shoot daggers when she overheard Mary Virginia say, "three?" Yes, three. Isn't it a tragedy to have lost three children? David, Carrie, and now Cathy. "Carrie?" Mary Virginia said. "Who told you that?" A funeral hardly seemed like a place to talk about dead people, so the topic was dropped. The casket was lowered.

The flowers had begun to wilt, the mourners had long since dispersed, and Mary Virginia had successfully slipped away without much notice. The audience was assembled at the foot of the bed Mrs. Carlson had taken to. Dirty dishes that had piled up on the bed next to her were cleared away. She'd not left this room in at least a week.

"I don't know what Mary Virginia told you," she said, "but she's a liar." This proclamation was mere preamble.

"Is it a crime?" Mrs. Carlson demanded, "to grieve so deeply for my angel that I couldn't leave his gravesite?

Well. Is it?" The audience was in for a spirited soliloquy, they knew, so no answer was required.

"It wasn't my fault," she said, "it was not. So-what if I tried to make arrangements for my child's funeral?"

"Well. No, of course it wasn't," one brave audience member offered, "what else were you expected to do with the poor little baby?"

"You don't understand. You don't, you don't. That's why I never tell you anything. I'm not talking about David." This comment was directed at no one in particular. Mrs. Carlson cast her eyes downward, allowing tears to drip instead of roll.

"There's no shame," she continued, after taking an unexceptionally light draw on her newly lit cigarette, "there's no shame in staying in a facility to get some rest after trying to cope with the loss of one child and the understandable mistake of trying to arrange to bury a child who wasn't, well, you know." She implied the child was a girl, but made no mention of "Sharon." It would take another twelve years for her name to be revealed.

Death upon death, grieving a different time and a different place; Mrs. Carlson spoke as if she'd not just buried Cathy, as if she were still only a loving mother of three.

Upon her release from the "facility," Mrs. Carlson was once again confronted with loss, she said. Doug had surreptitiously whisked their remaining two children away to an undisclosed location in his home state, thousands of miles away. He was a spindly man whom she knew wasn't a strong man, not like her father, who was made of steel and hardened concrete. Mrs. Carlson never saw the children again. Her beloved father passed away a few years later. The loss was becoming innumerable.

"What?!" Mary Virginia's voice crackled over the telephone line; her harrumph of fatigued indignation had become as predictable as Mrs. Carlson's disjointed

soliloquies. "No, no, no, sugar. Doug and the kids stayed in

town for years after that. Good Lord o' mine," she hastened

with a quick cackle, "you can't trust a word that comes out

of that woman's mouth."

Even their own father, Mrs. Carlson's white knight,

wasn't the Italian land baron whose twin had stolen all of

his property, forcing him to flee to American, where he

settled down in Richmond to rebuild his considerable

fortune. But that's where the talent of the liar lies, isn't it?

Weave just enough truth into a story to make it plausible.

Yes, their father was from Italy. Yes, he'd immigrated to

Virginia. The businesses? The fortunes? The twin? Lie.

Lie. Lie. In fact, their father was an only child.

Truth: one of his last acts before he passed away was

to keep Mrs. Carlson out of jail after her cross-country

Space Needle folly. It had been either the third or fourth

time, Mary Virginia couldn't remember exactly which, where he'd stepped in to help her.

"Let me get this straight," one audience member asked, "ok, so if Sharon was two when David was buried, then who was Carrie and how did she die?" Those pale green eyes once again did what they did; they shot daggers.

"You," Mrs. Carlson said. "You don't know me. You don't know me at all." She stubbed out her cigarette, hard, and reached for another one, her mood souring.

"You have no idea what I've been through." Unexpected proclamation, remember, equals preamble, so pay attention.

"There was a birthday party at my Aunt Harriet's farm," she said, after taking a moment to compose herself; her voice now calm and metered. "I had to drive into town to get the birthday cake. They had one of those fences that you drive up to, get out and open, drive through, and then go back and latch the gate. Understand? Good. It was just about dark when I got back with the cake and I didn't know anything about the prison break." She continued uninterrupted despite this seeming non sequitur.

"I got to the fence, went to open the gate to go through and..."

And that was when two escaped convicts, one white man and one black man, jumped her. "I was left for dead," she said, her southern accent trickling back as she recounted the scene. "The only reason anyone came lookin' for me was because they wanted to know where their damned cake was. They found me after they made sure the cake was okay." The calm in her voice had risen into anger when relating the detail of the cake, but soon descended back into her measured tone, growing quieter and more resolved.

Speaking in a near whisper now, she continued: "and through all the surgeries, through all the broken bones, the broken eye socket, the wired jaw. I was... I was still... I was still pregnant."

The assumption, though not confirmed, was this was more than likely the origin story of "Carrie." It was a gripping tale, told with just the right amount of intrigue and dramatic pauses. The audience was transported to Aunt Harriet's farm, right around dusk, where Mrs. Carlson had been savagely beaten and raped. There were tears all around now. Mrs. Carlson and the audience alike were all swept up in this harrowing tale. Swept up, that is, until the unexpected question was voiced.

"Was the baby white or half black?"

"What?!" Mrs. Carlson spat sharply, her eyes darting around the room, caged, trapped. Stammering, she said: "Wwwhhhite of COURSE."

As far as liars went, Mrs. Carlson was one of the best. Her stories typically ended with the audience going to the store for her, cleaning something, or lending her money.

But this time she'd blundered. She'd gotten cocky, maybe, gave too many details. The tears evaporated and the audience got up and left unceremoniously, the proverbial scales having fallen from their eyes.

When pressed for corroboration of this harrowing assault, Mary Virginia, harrumph, had no memory of anything remotely resembling this.

"Would escape convicts really leave a running car?" She asked. Harrumph, indeed.

It was 1994 now, two years later. The phone message, frantic and breathless, "my daughter's dead. My daughter is dead. Call me." The audience deleted the message. The slew of repeated calls went unanswered for several hours. In the 14 years since Cathy's death, sometimes Mrs. Carlson liked to pretend she didn't know Cathy was dead in order to relive the night the police came to her door to inform her. The hyperventilation. The

.

trembling. The blubbering. The appeal for comfort and support.

"No. MY daughter," Mrs. Carlson clarified, "IS dead."

Click.

The phone rang again.

Again. Dead daughter blah blah blah.

Click.

"My daughter, Sharon, not Cathy" Mrs. Carlson said in one loud blurt to her audience before the line could go dead again, "they just called me. She's been killed. In a car crash. In Oklahoma. Come quickly."

And with that, a lie miraculously turned into a truth. The count really did go to three: ~~David~~. ~~Cathy~~. ~~Sharon~~.

Reconnecting the awful present with the distant past upon Sharon's actual passing, there were some questions that were answered, and some that were not. Michael had been of draft age and left no trail, so only conjecture remains for him. For convenience's sake, let's add him to the "dead" category. This brings our count to four. In order: David, Cathy, Michael, Sharon. Dead. Dead. Dead. Dead.

Only Carrie remains an unsolved mystery child of this loving mother of five. Carrie's father could have been Janet Leigh's brother, or he could have been a correctional officer in a jail that housed Mrs. Carlson after her father helped get her a reduced sentence on some fraud charges, or it could have been anyone, save for an imaginary prison escapee. The cake and the gate might have been true, but there was nothing else about the story that even came close to reality.

All accounted for to varying degrees now, these are the five children of their loving mother, Mrs. Carlson: [Michael / Sharon / David]. [Carrie]? [Cathy].

One of Sharon's first memories, Mary Virginia said, was of Mrs. Carlson walking down a hallway, carrying a pillow. Could Mrs. Carlson have been a murderer as well as a liar as well as a thief? Was Sharon really only two when David died? Was it even her birthday? Could Mary Virginia be trusted to tell the truth?

What a sordid tale from such a sordid life.

When ordered to "come quickly" the night of Sharon's death, the audience abstained. The audience refused to sit through another farce. The audience, all along, had been Mrs. Carlson's youngest child, number 6, the one who didn't matter: the witness to her madness, the victim of her delusions, the child who never loved her, the child she never loved for want of those she'd lost. Cathy and I were full siblings, two years apart. Only fifteen years old, Mrs. Carlson had called upon me to identify Cathy's limp and blooded body.

John was father to both Cathy and me. My name is Georgia Gale Giggle, but you're welcome to continue thinking of me as "the audience," if you so please. John Giggle was a safe cracker who'd met Mrs. Carlson when

they both landed in Washington D.C.'s St. Elizabeth's
Hospital for the Criminally Insane in 1962, not long after
Mrs. Carlson had returned from Seattle. The four-digit bill
racked up by her extravagant cross-country check-writing
excursion to the World's Fair was no match for the double-
digit amount of money she'd deposited into a new checking
account just before setting out. There was just something
about getting up high enough to look down on the world
that was too enticing for her to pass up.

My parent's time together was relatively brief. They
never married, despite her referring to him as her fourth
husband. John died in 1994 at the age of 62. That's how far
four packs a day and a hair trigger temper will get you in
this world. He did not attend Cathy's funeral. I did not
attend his.

Mrs. Carlson, as it turns out, wasn't even her real
name. Someone said she'd taken it as some sort of homage
to an obscure architect I'd never heard of. This loving

mother of five, or whoever she was, is gone now as well.

seventy-something. Diabetic. Smoker. Hypochondriac. I

heard about her passing third- or fourth-hand, but can't

remember from where exactly. We'd lost touch long ago. It

was the only logical conclusion of an unmitigated disgust

and the hope of self-preservation. Mere mortals such as us,

it turns out, are no match for the beatified memories of the

saints who had graced this Earth before us.

Printed in Dunstable, United Kingdom